The Creative Writer

Level Three: Building Your Craft

Cover design by Mollie Bauer

Publisher's Cataloging-In-Publication Data (prepared by the Donohue Group, Inc.)

Fishman, Boris, 1979-

The creative writer. Level three, Building your craft / by Boris Fishman.

p. : ill. ; cm.

"... designed to be used in a mentor/student relationship, with teaching, guidance, and evaluation tips provided for the mentor or teacher."--Publisher's e-mail communication.

Interest grade level: 5-8.

ISBN: 978-1-933339-57-3

1. Creative writing (Elementary education) 2. Creative writing (Middle school) 3. English language--Composition and exercises--Study and teaching (Elementary) 4. English language--Composition and exercises--Study and teaching (Middle school) I. Title. II. Title: Building your craft

LB1576 .F57 2012b

372.62/3 2012912535

For a complete list of history, grammar, reading, and writing materials produced by Peace Hill Press, or to request a catalog, visit **peacehillpress.com**.

The Creative Writer

Level Three: Building Your Craft

by Boris Fishman

PEACE HILL PRESS
CHARLES CITY, VA

INTRODUCTION

TO THE STUDENT

This is the third volume in the four-volume *The Creative Writer* series. The last volume, *Level Two*, focused on the basic elements of fiction: plot, character, dialogue, setting, point of view. That is, a story needs to be *about something*—what happens in it is the **plot**. And, of course, it needs **characters** to whom this "something" is happening. These characters will probably talk to each other (**dialogue**); the story will probably take place somewhere (**setting**); and it will be narrated from the perspective of a particular character, who may or may not be part of the action, and may or may not be a trustworthy guide to the events of the story (**point of view**). These are the Five Essentials of a short story; practically every traditional short story will have them.

This year, we're going to get more detailed. Instead of dealing with these broad categories, we'll talk more about **technique**—that is, writing skills that make stories better. For instance, in Weeks 5–7, we'll talk about the difference between specific (**concrete**) and not very specific (**abstract**) descriptions of people, objects, settings, etc. In weeks 8–10, we'll work on **precision**—that is, on being ever more detailed, accurate, and articulate in our **concrete** descriptions. Weeks 11–13 focus on writing stories by **showing** all the action versus **explaining** (or telling) what everything that happens means.

This year's overall focus will be on character because, in some ways, it's the most important element of fiction. Some teachers of writing go so far as to say that "character is plot," by which they mean that a writer finds his plot by figuring out what happens to the characters he's created in the situation in which he's placed them. A shy, self-effacing guy and a brash, outspoken girl meet on the bench outside the principal's office—he, waiting to get enrolled in the school; she, on her way to detention. Not much plot here, except what the author comes up with based on the personalities of the characters he's working with.

If you're not already familiar with the Five Essentials of fiction, you might want to go back and complete the exercises in Level Two of *The Creative Writer.* But if you understand the basics of how these elements work, keep going.

Like fiction, poetry has 5 Essentials. In the second level of this series, we started with the question of **what to write about** (Weeks 1–4). Then we discussed **how** to write about it: **description** (Weeks 10–13). Then we moved on to **form**: how to organize a poem into lines and groups of lines called stanzas (Weeks 14–17). And we finished by discussing, just as in a song, **rhythm and sound**—how, for instance, the repetition of certain sounds or words affects the feelings inspired by a poem in the reader. (Weeks 14–17).

This year, we're going to study these elements again, but at a much faster clip. Instead of devoting a whole multi-lesson **unit** to each of the craft skills above—description, form, sound, etc.—we are going to devote only a single lesson to each. And instead of practicing these skills by writing poems of our own, we're going to do it by working with a published poem by a great American poet.

Her name is Sharon Olds. Born in 1942, she's one of America's greatest living poets. Olds writes vivid, honest poetry likely to stay with you long after you've finished it. Take "Feared Drowned," the poem that's going to be our focus for the next seven weeks. It features powerful descriptions; startling, unexpected comparisons; tremendous feeling and intelligence; and a look and sound that, in subtle ways, reinforce the main message of the poem.

At its most basic, the poem is about a woman on a beach who can't find her husband—hence the title. But as you'll see in the closing lines, which Olds uses to such powerful effect, this poem is also about a lot more than someone's afternoon on a beach. (As I mentioned last year, closing lines count for a lot because they're the last thing to stay with the reader.)

As in earlier volumes of the series, each lesson comes with additional guidance and direction for a mentor who can help you to make your work better.

TABLE OF CONTENTS

Fiction

FICTION SECTION 3 • PRECISION

FICTION SECTION 4 • SHOW AND TELL

FICTION SECTION 5 • GETTING AWAY FROM YOURSELF

FICTION SECTION 6 • STORY UNIT

Poetry

POETRY SECTION I • CRAFT PRACTICE USING A PUBLISHED POEM

POETRY SECTION 2 • THE FUNDAMENTALS, WITHOUT TRAINING WHEELS

POETRY SECTION 3 • BACK TO NONSENSE

POETRY SECTION 4 • FREE POEM UNIT

FICTION

FICTION • SECTION 1

CHARACTER REFRESHER AND BEYOND

WEEKS 1–4

RIFFING ON AN EXISTING CHARACTER

Purpose: To refresh our understanding of character by practicing on an already existing character, from fiction and real life.

Let's ease into things by filling out character profiles for characters who already exist. There was an exercise built around this in Level 2, but there, it was up to you to come up with a character you knew—someone from your neighborhood, say—and imagine her in an invented situation. This time, I'm going to provide a bit more guidance. This exercise has two parts. In the first, you're going to choose a *famous person* and imagine him in an invented situation.

What does "famous" mean? You can pick a historical and no-longer-alive figure like Abraham Lincoln or George Washington. Or you can pick a Hollywood actor, a singer, or a sports figure. The point is that it has to be someone publicly known, but whom you don't know personally.

Let's say you're interested in swimming and choose Michael Phelps, the swimmer who won all that gold at the Beijing Olympics in 2008. Your job is to imagine Michael Phelps in an invented situation. That is, if you watched the Olympics, you saw Phelps in the pool and maybe in the locker rooms during an interview; maybe the TV network did some kind of special highlighting his life and training back at home. Fine—but your job is to imagine Phelps in some *other* setting. Imagine him getting a phone call from a friend in need of help. Based on what you've seen about Phelps on TV, read in the newspapers, or discussed with your parents, siblings, and friends, what would he do?

The mission here is to depart from what you know about Phelps. That doesn't mean imagining the opposite of what you've observed about him. If the television special described him as humble and hard-working, you don't have to represent him as conniving and selfish. Rather, you have to extend the idea you have of the character into a situation in which you haven't observed him. If he's humble and hardworking, how would that shape his response to his friend?

As you do this, you'll want to keep in mind that even star athletes like Phelps are complicated characters because they're human, which means that they're imperfect. Listening to Michael be a goody two-shoes as he misses practice in order to advise his friend may be nice, but it's not going to make for compelling fiction. We want to go beyond the simplified portrait we get of politicians, actors, celebrities, and so on in the public arena. We want to learn who these people are in private.

Most people are neither good nor bad, but a mixture of the two, different parts of them gaining the upper hand at different moments. Also, we have public selves and private selves, and they don't always agree, especially if people have expectations of us in the public arena that we feel obligated to satisfy. (You'll practice creating characters with internal contradictions more next year.) So let us see your favorite football player, your favorite actor, or your favorite historical or scientific figure in a private setting.

Another example: If you picked the president of the United States—someone you've probably observed a great deal at state functions, and wearing a suit—you might imagine him on a fishing trip. What is he wearing? What kind of tics/habits/pet peeves does he have? What kind of character traits does he reveal during the outing? Who is with him? Where have they gone to fish? What happens? As we've learned, it's hard to come up with a character profile for someone without touching on other aspects of a short story.

Unlike last year, when your character profile consisted of 500 words in narrative form or as bullet-point entries (essentially, you *told* us who this person was), this year, I'd like you to try to ***show*** **who the character is by writing a 500-word scene featuring a situation, dialogue, description of a setting, etc.** That is, don't say "President So-and-so likes to joke around." That's too abstract for this assignment. Instead, write something like:

The lake was up a series of switchbacks on a dried-out mountain, their main company the periodic marmot burrowing into the scree. The water glistened with a painful blue. As they unloaded and pushed off, a golden eagle swooped down low over the water, making its crik-crak.

They were out for nearly an hour when Cutty, the Secret Service man, announced he didn't have this kind of patience and started digging around in the cooler. While Cutty was turned around, the President pulled up Cutty's line, replaced the bait on its hook with a small cantaloupe he had been hoarding, and released it into the water.

"Whoa, Cutty, you got one, you got one—you've got to pay attention!" the President shouted.

Cutty tossed half the cooler overboard getting his hand back on the rod and wheeling it up with all fury. When the yellow melon popped out of the water, everybody burst into laughter.

"I wouldn't have done it if I'd known you'd throw our lunch overboard," the President sighed.

The above fragment is only 170 words, so you can devote more room to details like setting and dialogue, which figure briefly above. (Notice also the use of precise, specialized, "technical" language: "switchbacks," "scree," etc. Also, "crik-crak" is an example of something we haven't discussed yet: **onomatopoeia**, which refers to the use of words that describe a sound by imitating it.)

A BRIEF NOTE ABOUT SHOWING VS. TELLING:

We'll talk a lot more about the difference between showing and telling later this year, but here is a brief introduction. My little excerpt nowhere tells the reader that the president is a prankster. Instead, it describes an episode during which the president *acts* like a prankster. Sometimes the author *tells* us that a character is, say, petulant; sometimes, she *shows* us, by having a character whine on about something or other.

Showing does not have to take the form of dialogue and presented action. Consider the following:

> They rowed for a quarter of an hour, losing sight of the shoreline. Cutty thought the rowboat was tilting right, so he went into the cooler, meaning to shift some of the contents to the front. While he was dug in back there, lifting out Ziploc bags of chili and rice, the President reached out two fingers and began to reel in Cutty's line. When he had the hook in hand, he slipped off the rubber worm and hooked the cantaloupe that he had stashed in his gym bag. It dropped to the bottom of the lake so fast that Cutty's rod nearly went overboard. The President yelled and Cutty lunged for it, a couple of Ziplocs flying out of his hands into the lake. When he hauled up the brick of the melon, you could hear the laughter all the way back at the shore.

This fragment shows through **description by the author** rather than by **dialogue**. But still, it *shows* rather than *tells*. It never directly spells out the "message" behind the presentation: the President is a prankster.

Your turn. Remember: 500 words, featuring a situation, dialogue, description of a setting, and so on, all of it designed to show who a character *is*.

CHALLENGE EXERCISE

1. Do something similar for an existing but *fictional* character whom you're drawn to: Elizabeth Bennet from *Pride and Prejudice*, Harry Potter, Ender Wiggin from Orson Scott Card's *Ender's Game.*

2. Place the character you choose in a situation in which the book or film in question hasn't placed him or her. Then show or tell us about the character in the situation. The same rules apply: Write a scene of 500 words, where the qualities of the character are entirely up to you.

CHARACTER FROM SCRATCH

Purpose: To refresh our recollection of how to create characters from scratch.

This week, you're going to write another five-hundred-word scene that shows who a character is. However, before you write the scene, you need to perform a couple of extra steps.

In previous levels of this series, I recommended that you start keeping a notebook so that you have a treasure trove of ready material—funny sayings, memorable details, observed character tics—when you sit down to write a story and need details to get your imagination going.

Next time you're in line at the supermarket, I want you to pull out the little notebook in which you write down your interesting observations. In this notebook, make notes about the person(s) directly in front of you and directly behind you. Write down whatever you think is important—what they're wearing, the expressions on their faces, what they're holding, what their relationships are to each other, what they might be thinking about.

When you're back home, I want you tell us more about these people. Like a private investigator, I want you to tail them (in your imagination!) to their homes or wherever they go after the supermarket. I want you to show us what their lives are like.

Your second step is to sketch character portraits for the main players. First, how many are there? If you took notes about a couple, you'll have two. You can write about both, or you may wish to focus on only one member of the pair. Write down 10 adjectives that describe each subject. Then, come up with three different situations that exhibit their character. (Do they sneak down to the fridge at midnight? Go fishing or to the opera on the weekends? What's their favorite magazine?)

Which of the three situations feels the most interesting or promising? In other words, which one gives you the most ideas on what happens next? Choose that one.

Now you're at the final step: Develop the situation into a 500-word scene involving the chosen character(s).

Note that you're not writing a *story* about these individuals—that is, you don't have to come up with a **plot** that features **conflict** or **suspense**. These characters don't have to have a **quest**, except what emerges naturally from your description/presentation of them. I simply want you to zero in on the individuals in question, and tell us, step by step, for 500 words, what you envision them wearing, doing, and thinking.

You will be demonstrating their characters by means of **showing** or **telling**. If you give us their **dialogue** and **action**s without a great deal of explanation, you'll be mostly **showing**. If you describe their **dialogue** and **action** in your own voice, you'll still be **showing** them to us, but through a more **tell**-heavy approach. Your third option, of course, is simply to **tell** us critical information about these characters. As you'll learn more formally in the show vs. tell unit, for which this unit is meant to be a practice run, pure telling doesn't work if that's all you do for a whole story—it leaves nothing to the reader's imagination, and can get quite abstract. ("Mindy was sad." Sad *how*?) But you can't only write scenes, either, as that can get quite laborious and lengthy. The best writers use both tools. Knowing when to use which is the great talent that writers work a long time to develop, and what we'll be practicing throughout this year.

Before you get started, read through the following examples for a little additional guidance.

1. SHOWING-THROUGH-TELLING:

> They loaded the grocery bags into the trunk; Mindy dumped hers, earning a scowl from her father. Their mint-green Honda touched off slowly. Mindy's father always said you saved the most gas if you accelerated gradually. On those rare days when Mindy had the car to herself, she

gunned it with everything the little two-door had. Now, she sat quietly in the passenger seat as her father told her again: Slow when the light changes. Every little bit counts, Mindanao. His stupid nickname for her. It was some island in the Philippines. Her dad burned a whole lot more electricity watching the History Channel than she did gas running the car. But he never turned his big-saver eye on himself. And how many times did he have to tell her to keep it slow when the light changed?

This car has barely left the supermarket parking lot! I used every little thing that happens when a car pulls out of a parking spot at the supermarket—bags of groceries, gas pedal, etc.—to think of *how* Mindy and her dad might feel about it.

In this type of showing, all the information is presented by the author. But he isn't just telling us that "Mindy is annoyed with her father" or that "Mindy's father is frugal." He is showing us by *telling* us what Mindy is thinking: she is fuming about her father constantly warning her to accelerate slowly so as not to waste gas.

(The example I just gave you draws the character of Mindy and her father from Mindy's perspective, by telling us what Mindy's thoughts are. So here's a pop quiz: Is this a first- or third-person narration? You're right if you answered third—a narrator is telling us the story, not Mindy. But you'll agree that this is a pretty all-knowing narrator if he can climb so deeply into Mindy's secret thoughts. There's a name for a third-person narrator with this kind of access—a ***close* third-person narrator**. Hopefully the terminology makes sense: It's a third-person narrator with very close access to a character's thoughts. More on this in this level's lesson on various kinds of point of view.)

2. PURE SHOWING

Here's another way to do this assignment:

> The mint-green Honda touched off.
>
> "The toy store first, honey?" Tami said.
>
> "I need to change the oil," Eric answered.
>
> "If you take that shortcut on Alps, we'll pass the toy store first."
>
> "If I don't take the shortcut, we'll pass the gas station first."
>
> "I'm not buying the toy for me, Eric. I'm buying it for our child. Our child. My child and your child."
>
> "A hundred dollars for a bear that sings?"
>
> "That's rich. It's the kid's birthday. How many times a year do you change that oil at twenty bucks a pop? Rick next door does it himself. He'd do it for you at half price if you asked him."
>
> "I don't exactly use this car for joy-riding," Eric said, pointing at the baby seat in the back.

Here, we have a couple quite obviously involved in a passive-aggressive argument even though the author never tells us that. Does this behavior suggest any permanent personality characteristics of either? Deeper problems in the relationship? If this were your assignment, you'd have 369 more words to build out these characters and let us know.

The information is revealed not through the narrator's description, but through dialogue, with little explanatory context from the narrator. He's not telling us anything—he's just reporting what is being said. We may be witnessing a couple on the verge of divorce or a typical weekend spat indicative of nothing overly serious. The narrator doesn't elaborate for us, and while we can deduce a good deal from the signals in this segment, we need to see more before we arrive at conclusions.

You'll notice that this narrator isn't "close" in the way of the first excerpt; he's simply transcribing the dialogue, giving us no clues to the private thoughts of the characters. He could be sitting in the back seat with "record" pushed on his recorder.

3. A COMBINATION OF SHOWING AND SHOWING-THROUGH-TELLING

Here's a final example, rendering some of the same information as the first (and some of the plot details of the second), through a combination of **showing** and **showing-through-telling**.

> They turned off Berdan and headed to the mall. Their little mint-green Honda had looked hideous since Mindy had kissed the rear end of a parked Pathfinder on a recent snowy night. It had been hailing so hard she could barely see inside the car, let alone past it. Her father parked at the far edge of the mall lot, so no one would see. Everyone in town knew that Honda by its color. Mint Chocolate Chip, Mindy's classmates called it when she drove to school. Little Green Giant.
>
> They tried Nuts for Tots, but even a talking bear was a hundred dollars. "Con artists," Mindy's father growled. At Serious Munchkins, they had a 2-for-1, but who could afford even the 1? Finally, at Big Bright Sunshine, Mindy's father strode up to the clerk and said, "What if you just give us some of that wrapping paper you use for the gifts? They ran out at the other store." Mindy looked away. The clerk handed it over, raising his hand to say: No charge.
>
> "Let's see what your mother remembers from that origami class," Mindy's father said as they crossed the parking lot back to the car.

This form of showing combines the more explanatory style of the first segment—though it still doesn't tell the reader something explicit like "Mindy's father was concerned about appearances"—with some of the unexplained action that dominated the second example up above.

What do I mean by unexplained action? Simply, the narration doesn't go into a great deal of justification or context. Take, for instance, the phrase "...parked it at the edge of the lot." There is no explanatory follow-up such as "No way to fix it until his bonus came in from the shop at the end of the month. He knew half the town would be at the mall now, and he had no great desire to show how the Smiths were doing on this eve of the holiday season."

The narration above stays pretty much on the surface, mostly giving us the play-by-play and hoping we can understand the message between the lines. This happened, then that happened.

As for character, the individual personalities here become less noticeable than the general struggle of their lives. You could say the character here is the family rather than the individuals. Even so, we can tease out that the father, while perhaps irritable, loves his family and wants whoever the gift is for—probably Mindy's younger sibling – to have something. Meanwhile, Mindy is embarrassed about having such reduced means. Her father is concerned about appearances, too—he claims to have bought a gift at the other store so his request for the wrapping paper doesn't seem paltry – so maybe it runs in the family.

Now, it's your turn.

CHALLENGE EXERCISES

1. There are lots of other ways to do this exercise. Draw a character for your reader using the perspective of a first-person narrator. The described character could be the narrator herself, or merely someone observed by the narrator.

2. Write one of the scenes above from the perspective of another character, using either close third-person or first-person narration. Mindy's dad might be a wise, angelic man, if we don't have to view him through Mindy's eyes!

AGAINST TYPE

Purpose: To create characters who don't fit expectations.

We all know what stereotypes are: Simplistic ideas about types of people, such as "all cops eat donuts," "all jocks are dumb," "old people are crabby." Some might argue they serve a useful purpose—a usually correct shortcut to figuring out how you feel about someone without having to spend time to get to know them. I couldn't disagree more. Everyone—everyone—is interesting, surprising, and complex. It's your job—as a human being and, especially, as a writer—to dig down and find that complexity. Sometimes, the interesting bits might be unknown even to the person in question—some people play into stereotypes because it's what's expected of them—but that doesn't mean that you have to go along.

One of a writer's most important—and interesting—obligations is to create characters who go **against type**. That doesn't mean creating characters who are the *opposite* of type (an old man who jumps off cliffs, or a pitcher for the Cleveland Indians who is also a Ph.D. in molecular biology). Don't get me wrong—those characters would be interesting, but they would also be exceptional. Fiction works to disprove stereotypes, but not by demonstrating their opposite; rather, it aims to describe people in all the richness of their selves—their ideas, quirks, fears, etc.

Let me give you an example. Recently, I was sitting in a café (working on this book!). It was early afternoon, when most people are at work, so I was surrounded by senior citizens—an elderly couple (both of them with walkers) and about a half-dozen of their friends (all male). The men were arguing about baseball while the woman sat quietly. The part of my brain used to stereotypes immediately jumped to conclusions: Men talk about sports, and women don't. That was when the woman finally spoke up. And not only did she speak up, but she delivered a set of opinions about various players and team prospects that put the men to shame!

This is what I mean by **against type**. The elderly woman who's a whiz about baseball; the captain of the football team who introduces himself to the shy, new girl in school; the airline pilot who joined up not because he's fearless and always dreamed of flying, but precisely because he's terrified of heights and hoped to overcome it this way—all these are characters who defy type.

Have you ever watched the television show *Friday Night Lights*? Every character on that show both embodies type and defies it. The coach, Eric Taylor, can get gruff and loud, but he's a soft touch at home, and at heart he deeply loves and cares for his players. His wife is a responsible mom and takes care of some traditional duties at home, but she is also a career woman who's risen to principal of Dillon High School. Tim Riggins, the fullback, embodies some of the worst stereotypes of a dumb jock, except that he can also be tender, nervous, shy, and generous.

Creating characters who work against type isn't the same as creating characters who harbor contradictions. We'll do that next year. Simply, it means figuring out the ways in which they depart from cultural norms like "senior citizen," "jock," or "mom."

Your job this week is to create a character who goes **against type**. You don't have to write a full scene featuring this character. Instead, you can *describe* the scene you would write or the person in question.

Here's an example, using my baseball-expert pensioner:

> Barbara Gold is 76 and has gout, which requires her to use a walker. It's an especially embittering illness for her because as a girl, she used to run marathons. In her hometown in New Jersey, she was the first woman to have ever run a marathon alongside the men. Now, she is reduced to spectatorship. She doesn't care so much what she watches—baseball with her husband, curling with her son, football with her grandson. She just loves her sports. Once, when she and Marc, her grandson, were watching the Jets, Barbara shared her mind about the quarterback's throwing arm, how it compared to his predecessor, and why the team was completely failing to utilize the man's height. The boy was shocked. At his college, he helped run a website devoted to professional sports. He came to his editor-in-chief with the world's greatest idea: His grandmother, blogging. Just give her a shot, he pleaded. It was crazy enough that the editor-in-chief went for it. Monday mornings now, Marc calls up Grandma and writes down what she has to say about Sunday night's game, transcribing it word for word, including the cussing. Within a month, she had 10,000 readers.

Barbara Gold is a typical pensioner in many ways: Her health is failing, her movement is limited, and, well, she's a bit crabby about those football players. However, she is also an avid sports fan and a budding blogger! Not things you expect to hear about a 76-year-old woman on a walker. (Notice also that even though I started with nothing more than a series of facts about Barbara in narrative form, they inevitably steered me toward the premise of a story: Barbara as a blogger.)

Your turn. **In 250 words, create a character who runs against type.** Do so in narrative form—as opposed to bullet points—as I have above with my baseball-whiz pensioner.

CHALLENGE EXERCISE

1. Write a scene—using dialogue, action, and so forth (look back at Week 2 for examples)—that demonstrates the kind of person your against-type character is.

A CONFLICT BETWEEN TWO EQUALLY SYMPATHETIC CHARACTERS

Purpose: To try your hand at a more complicated character exercise.

In Level Two of this series, I asked you to create characters on a quest but opposed by some kind of force. They were a basketball team playing bigger, better rivals. They wanted to go to college in another state, but their parents said no. For the most part, our sympathies were with the questing character, not the force standing in their way. But real life doesn't split so neatly into good guys and bad. As I've mentioned several times now, all of us contain a little bit of both, which emerge at different moments, depending on a variety of circumstances. It's the job of fiction to represent this, because you never want your reader to throw your story down with exasperation because it's a fairy-tale version of reality.

This week you're going to practice creating a situation in which two equally sympathetic characters are pitted against each other. That is, you're going to have two **protagonists**—the main characters in a story—with redeeming characteristics that make the reader want to root for both of them. Imagine you have two players meeting in the finals of a sport, be it tennis or a dance competition. Many stories would side with one, telling the story from her perspective and subtly making us root for her triumph. (You'll remember from a couple of weeks ago that this would be called **close third-person narration**. We would be *close* to one of the characters. If you want to jump ahead and review close narration before returning to this lesson, you can do that in Week 14.)

Your challenge this week is different: Devote that kind of narrative attention and sympathy-creating detail to both characters.

How might you do that? Well, you can flip back and forth between the perspectives of the contestants, but that alone isn't enough, because that still allows you to make one of our tennis players—let's stick with that example—good-hearted and the other calculating and mean. You have to reveal something about each of the characters that makes us want both of them to win. Obviously, it's impossible for both of them to win, but it's the kind of heart-rending conflict that makes us want to read on, to find out what happens. Even if the story's going to break our heart, it's so powerful and moving that we want to keep reading. That power comes from the push and pull of feeling sympathy for both contestants.

This exercise will force you to refresh some skills you developed before: How do we get readers to like or dislike our characters? In the fairy tale "Rapunzel," by the Brothers Grimm, we see the prince who woos Rapunzel being kind, devoted, and unfairly punished—all things that made us sympathize with him. This kind of innocent, virtuous do-gooding works better in fairy tales than in modern short stories; if one of your tennis players is a goody two-shoes who always cleans her room and has never misbehaved, that might be a little boring, leading us to root for the other person. The way to engage a reader isn't to make her a "saint"; the reader won't recognize himself or herself in such a person. It's much more compelling—and honest—to draw a character who teems with all the contradictions of a real-life person.

Your mission, as in Weeks 1 and 2 this year, is to **write a 500-word scene. This week, the scene should present to the reader two equally sympathetic characters who are engaged in some kind of conflict.** The conflict doesn't have to be literal: you can have two players on a tennis court. Or you can have two individuals who want conflicting things: say, a loving father who is also a football coach with an incredible coaching opportunity in another state, and a daughter who wants to stay in town where she has made so many friends and found a sense of home (a storyline from *Friday Night Lights*).

Here's an example using our tennis players:

Sandra Guerrero tied and re-tied her shoes as she watched the doubles final run its course on the locker-room television. Her heart was trying to jump out of her throat. Her first singles final. She had thought about this day since she was old enough to wrap her pink little paw around her father's wooden racquet. Now that it was here, that momentum felt as gone as everything she had learned playing tennis for the last 15 years. Her racquets were strange beasts lined up in the corner, scheming to betray her.

"Can I get you anything? Water?" An attendant was in the doorway.

"I'm trying to focus," Sandra snapped.

The attendant shook her head and stepped out.

Sandra flushed. She turned around to apologize – it was because she was embarrassed to be caught in such a state – but the attendant was gone, and the bitterness in Sandra's throat expanded.

Twenty feet down the hall, Eva Tarkington was doing push-ups. Her mind was racing, and the best way to chase that away was to get the body moving. Eighteen, nineteen, twenty. She decided to start over. She tried to visualize the final point, the tennis ball sailing over the net as Sandra Guerrero tried to reach it without success. That girl had the easiest draw on her way to the final. But shouldn't that mean that Eva ought to be feeling more confident than she was right now?

> Eva had a hard time revving herself up against Sandra Guerrero. Sandra Guerrero, whose father had taught her to play using a wooden racquet until she was 12. Whose father had died in a motorcycle accident on the eve of her first big tournament victory. Eva was surrounded by girls who had their careers handed to them by parents with big wallets and tennis academies that gave them free rides. Sandra wasn't like that. So, how in the word was Eva supposed to rev herself up to beat her?

Who do you want to win this match? I hope you're scratching your head. Sandra is no saint, having snapped at the attendant, but she's no monster either, immediately feeling bad for it, and generally exhibiting a nervousness that makes us want to wish her well.

Different things incline us in Eva's favor. She can be envious and dismissive— "that girl had the easiest draw on her way to the final" —but she also possesses the honesty to admit that Sandra is an honorable competitor who's worked really hard to get to the top.

In Level 1 of this series, I included an exercise that asked you to note an "L" (for Like) and a "D" (for Dislike) next to moments that made us like or dislike the Prince in "Rapunzel." Well, Sandra's nervousness makes us sympathize with her, and Eva's generosity to Sandra makes us sympathize with *her*. I'd put an L next to both of those moments, and D's next to Sandra's rudeness to the attendant, and next to Eva's jealousy of Sandra's easy draw.

There are many ways to create feelings of sympathy for a character: Have her do (or think) something nice for someone else; have someone be unfair to her; and so on. Conversely, there are just as many ways of creating antipathy, or dislike, for a character: Have her be mean to someone defenseless, have her be jealous, have her snap at an attendant only trying to help!

Your turn. Start by coming up with a situation involving two characters. They could be involved in a literal conflict, though they don't have to be. You may wish to sketch character portraits for them beforehand and decide on at least one "positive" and at least one "negative" trait for each character. Then bring these facts alive in your 500-word scene.

CHALLENGE EXERCISES

1. Go a step further and take a peek into the next level of this series. Write a scene involving characters who are not only equally sympathetic, but who are also complex—that is, both sympathetic and not very sympathetic. You saw hints of this in the excerpt above about Sandra and Eva. Sandra is excited and nervous, but prone to temper. Eva is generous toward Sandra, but can be envious and self-serving, too. Make these girls or your characters less appealing than they currently are.

2. Go even further and create a scene involving two characters who are both unsympathetic. The risk here is that you might create characters who are hard to care about, and the reader may get bored and put the story down. So, you must come up with something in the characters' personalities that will make us keep reading. The presence of a conflict or contest may not be enough. If we hate both Sandra and Eva, we don't care who's going to win their match. This is a preview of next year's exercise on anti-heroes, or characters who don't fit conventional ideas of "goodness," but who receive our readerly support anyway. Think about superheroes—they're usually not law-abiding, by-the-book defenders of justice, but we root for them because their hearts are in the right place. Even though they often have to resort to grisly means of enforcement, they employ them only against people who "deserve" it. This is also the premise behind television shows like "Dexter," about a serial killer who dispenses only with "deserving" victims, and "House," which features a brilliant doctor who can be really unkind to those around him.

I just watched *Butch Cassidy and the Sundance Kid* with Paul Newman and Robert Redford. They play outlaws who rob bank after bank for no purpose greater than their own spending; yet we root for them, not for the law enforcers after them. Partly because that law—in the figure of lawman Joe LeFors—is faceless. We never meet Joe, never learn anything about him that would remind us that he's a human being with his own reasons for doing what he does. That would have made a more morally complicated tale.

FICTION • SECTION 2

VIVID AND ORIGINAL PROSE

WEEKS 5-7

CONCRETE VS. ABSTRACT

Purpose: To learn how to describe originally and vividly.

With this description unit, we're going to go further than we did last year. We're going to start learning how to write originally and vividly. That is, we won't be merely observing something closely. We'll be using every descriptive tool in our arsenal—concrete (as opposed to abstract) language, smart comparisons, distinctive word choice, synonyms—*at once* to create writing that isn't only observant, but interesting, too.

Compare these two sentences:

> The weather was bad in Heathertown.
>
> Heathertown sat wedged into a cliffside that dropped into the ocean, so it was battered by rain and winds so gusty that the church had to replace its wooden belfry every spring.

Which sentence puts you in Heathertown more effectively? The second one, I'd bet. Part of it is the detail, available only to someone who's observed the place closely, but part of it is the language: "Wedged," not "located"; "dropped into the ocean," not "exposed to the ocean." Both **word choices** create a sense of vertiginous exposure much more effectively than their paler, more literal counterparts. (Don't know what "vertiginous" means? Look it up.)

Specificity counts for a lot here, too. Saying "the winds gusted viciously," which is vivid enough, is less effective than "so gusty that the church had to replace its wooden belfry every spring." Those details really place you there, and really make it hard to believe that this is made up (which is the illusion that fiction tries to create). Generalities, by virtue of being unspecific and not giving your mind something to lock onto and imagine, are hard to believe. **Concrete details**—you'll remember such details as **authenticating details** from last year—create an undeniable sense of reality. There will be more on authenticating details in the next section.

Take the word "sorrow." Is it concrete or abstract? You might be tempted to say concrete because you know that sorrow means sadness, and you know what that feels like. But isn't sorrow a pretty broad, general way of describing sadness? Sorrow can means sadness over a death in the family; it can mean sadness due to loneliness; it can mean many things. As I've mentioned in previous levels, there's a great test for whether something is concrete vs. abstract: Can you pour chocolate sauce on it? If you can't, it's abstract. Can you pour chocolate sauce on "blue"? No. But on a "blue cat"? Yes, indeed.

Compare "sorrow" to a word like "matchbox" or "giraffe" or even "tears." You can see "tears" in a way you can't see "sorrow." When you read the words "tears" in a story, it goes right to your heart in a way "sorrow" does not. "Sorrow" talks to your brain, but "tears" makes you feel something. "Sorrow" won't remind you of the last time you were sad; "tears" will remind you of a time when you or someone you care about cried. "Tears" is simply that much more immediate and sharp. "Sorrow" is hazy.

Your first assignment this week is to categorize words as either concrete or abstract. Pick a fresh page in your notebook, draw a thick line down the middle, and give the left column the heading "concrete" and the right column the heading "abstract."

Second, grab a dictionary and jot down the first twenty words you find.

Finally, choose a column for each word. Write each word under either "abstract" or "concrete," and then be ready to explain to your mentor exactly why you chose the column you did.

Don't worry about whether the words are nouns, verbs, adjectives, adverbs, etc. If you don't know the word, read the definition. And remember that there isn't an answer that's always right: "Flowers" are more concrete than "celebration," but less concrete than "azaleas."

Pay special attention to what the word makes you feel on first hearing: Does it prompt a strong, sharp, concrete image? Can you pour chocolate sauce on it? You can pour chocolate sauce on "diplomat," but you can't pour chocolate sauce on "diplomacy."

Make sure you justify each of your answers to your mentor.

Please keep in mind two more things:

> **1. Abstractions aren't evil. Sometimes, there's no way to avoid them. Rather, you should simply try to keep them to a minimum. Imagine that concrete words cost you a penny and abstract terms cost you a dollar.**
>
> **2. There are no hard-and-fast rules here. A lot of words can be abstract in one usage and concrete in another. "A parade of emotions" is abstract. "A parade of buglers" is concrete.**

I know that the distinctions may seem tough at this point, but this is a challenging aspect of writing. It will come with time. Don't get discouraged. Here's my stab at 20 words I found in the dictionary, followed by the explanations for why I classified each one as I did.

Words:
mole, herald, propel, reproof, tender, technology, raspberry, jab, jockey, flood, nutmeg, nutritious, parade, permeable, school, stanch, tendency, visit, zodiac, X-ray

concrete:

- mole
- herald (n.)
- raspberry
- jab
- jockey
- flood
- nutmeg
- parade
- school
- zodiac (if we're talking about a diagram of the astrological signs)
- x-ray

abstract:

- propel (could be referring to many different kinds of movement – a football? a spaceship?)
- reproof (Reproof is quite general; it's another word for "criticism." Imagine how much more effective "shout" or "slap" would be.)
- tender (Another borderline. Goes in the abstraction column because "tender" how? "She was tender" is abstract. "She swept her fingertips across his cheek" is concrete.)
- technology (Too broad. "Computer" is concrete; "technology" is abstract.)
- nutritious (Broad again. "Nutritious" how?)
- permeable (Borderline. Vivid enough to bring up the definition – porousness between two things – but which two things?)
- stanch (Same logic. "Stanch" what? Blood? That would be concrete. "Stanch" a flood? Concrete again. "Stanch" the flow of his ideas? Quite abstract, and not very good writing.)
- tendency
- visit (we'd need more information to judge whether it's concrete)

Now, your turn.

CHALLENGE EXERCISE

Rewrite the following 10 sentences concretely:

1. They were in love.
2. The sunset always brought him down.
3. It got dark.
4. The loud noise woke them.
5. They stared at the pale canvas.
6. Oh, she's such a lovely person.
7. Politics is a brutal profession.
8. That guy can be so mean.
9. The sky was blue.
10. I don't like bitter foods.

THE SEA SEVEN WAYS

Purpose: To practice a more complex kind of comparison.

If you think The Sea Seven Ways is a great new dish at the local Chinese restaurant, think again. It's a comparison exercise. In previous levels of this series, we compared one thing (the sea) to another (a big blue bowl). This week, you're going to look for more than one comparison for that original item. You're going to look for seven—one for every day of the week. To make life easier, pick an original item—the one for which you'll be finding comparisons—that changes appearance every day: the shape of the clouds in the sky, the waves in the ocean, etc. You could also choose something that doesn't necessarily change every day, but offers many examples of different shapes and appearances, like the woods. Then, each day, find something new to compare it to.

Here's an example: Last year, I was living on Cape Cod, in Massachusetts. The Atlantic Ocean—or, more accurately, Provincetown Harbor, which lets out onto Cape Cod Bay, which joins the Atlantic—was a block and a half from my doorstep. I tried to walk to it almost every day, even though it was winter. It was a beautiful, calming sight, especially on a clear day. The water looked completely different each time I saw it. The first time that I walked out to the beach, the sky was overcast. The water was rolling furiously toward the shore, each quick wave barely reaching shore before the next one was on its back. In my notebook, I wrote:

> Overcast: The sea is like a great gray tongue spitting/rolling/frothing out waves of foam, like spitting out shells of sunflower seeds.

On another day:

Bright and blue: The sea, coming in at an angle, is like a great blue canvas being stretched over a baseball diamond, a tennis court when there's rain, or a pool table.

A third day:

Bright but cold: The water is like a Rothko painting: silver bottom half, blue-gray top. Invisible droplets fall into the water, spreading out in concentric circles, like a pebble in a lake. (Mark Rothko painted paintings that appear to be divided into several blocks of solid color.)

And so forth. Here are a few more daily entries from my journal:

First sunny day in a week. Windy, the water barreling at an angle, like a river swollen by snowmelt. Like a head rushing with thoughts.

The sand looks as windswept and endless as the Sahara.

The stormy water is like a bowl with the milk spilling over the edges.

The water resembles a nervous dark sheet, green and gray, with tiny stipples of angry whitecaps.

The water is as still as a pane of glass, lapping as feebly as a brook.

As above, your comparisons don't have to be very long: a sentence or even a sentence fragment will do. But make sure it's an actual comparison ("looks like a pane of glass") rather than merely a description ("it's blue").

Now it's your turn. **Pick something which either changes appearance constantly (clouds, bodies of water) or whose appearance looks different whenever you look (the woods) and compare that appearance to something new every day for seven days. Write down each day's comparison!** At the end of the week, read all seven comparisons to your mentor. The comparisons can be one sentence long, or a paragraph—that's up to you.

If you're not sure what to pick, go with clouds. If you happen to have a couple of cloudless days this week, then make up for them by coming up with more than one comparison on the cloudy days. The nice thing about clouds is that they're changing shape *all* the time.

CHALLENGE EXERCISES

1. Nothing is what it is. Spend a week comparing everything you can to something else:

    The steam rising from the coffeepot to a smokestack above a nuclear plant; the rumbling of the dishwasher to a hungry stomach; the clatter of silverware in the sink to voices in a gallery. Make sure to compare at least 10 items a day to one other thing. Keep your list in a notebook.

2. Alternative: Have a mentor or friend/sibling provide you with 10 daily objects/actions for which to find comparisons.

3. Even though you're looking for new comparisons for the same thing each day, that thing is ever-changing in this exercise. Find seven comparisons for something that *doesn't* change every day, such as seven comparisons for the sound of a hummingbird's wings.

WORD CHOICE

Purpose: To produce vivid and original writing through picking exactly the right words.

At the beginning of Level One of this series, I talked about the differences in the verbs "throw," "lob," and "chuck." They all mean more or less the same thing, but that "more or less" is critical to the writer. "Throw" is generic, an "invisible" word; it doesn't draw much attention to itself. "Lob" is more specific, more vivid—it conjures a high arc. Tennis balls get lobbed, grenades get lobbed. "Chuck" has an undercurrent of derision or indifference; we chuck things about which we don't want to be particularly careful, either because we're bored or angry.

A typical short story will have several thousand words, and the best writers devote this kind of attention to selecting many of them. Don't think that they stop and draw up these kinds of analyses or anything; once they've started paying attention to the subtle differences between the meanings and sounds of words, the ability to choose more specific, vivid words becomes an instinct.

This week, your job will be to **rewrite a 300-word paragraph in more vivid, original language.** Your main goal is to find more specific, vivid words for the pale, literal options with which I provide you below, but you should feel free to deploy your other descriptive tools as well: Close detail, concrete language, sharp comparisons.

One important note: Exchanging a ten-cent word ("chew") for a ten-dollar synonym ("masticate") is NOT the point here. Overly fancy words are just that—overly fancy. In a story, they're somewhat embarrassing because they make it seem like the author is full

of himself, showing off. They should be used very selectively. More often than not, they stand out like someone in a ball gown at a car wash. Picking more *vivid* alternatives isn't the same as picking fancy ones. (Think of "exposed to the ocean" vs. "*dropped* into the ocean." There's nothing fancy about "dropped," but it's a lot more vivid than simple, literal "exposed.") In fact, "masticate" is far less vivid than "chew," since "masticate," being unknown to most readers, conjures nothing in the mind. "Chew," at least, definitely brings up an image of a mouth working away. You aren't required to exchange a word for only a single word. Your job is to say the same thing more vividly, and if that requires a couple of extra words, that's fine. If you're not sure whether you're succeeding, try out the original and your new phrasing on a test subject, like a parent or a sibling. Which variant sounds more vivid to him or her?

Then there are the words that shouldn't – can't – be switched out. There's no better way to say "chicken bone." Trying to come up with an alternative would sound silly and evasive. "Chicken bone" is concrete – you should stay with it.

Here's your paragraph. Let's stay with the subject of eating. For which words can you find better substitutes? Which phrases can you say in more interesting ways?

> I wish Kilroy had better manners at the table. He eats so impolitely. When we have neighbors over, my face gets red and I lose my appetite. He's a big guy, so it's hard to get him to do what you want. When the Halberts stopped by, Kilroy threw a chicken bone at Mrs. Halbert. She got redder than I did. "It's fine, it's just fine," she said, and laughed, and got up to go to the bathroom. My husband Pete hit Kilroy on the head with a broom. Oh well. That's when things really got out of hand. Kilroy kicked Pete, which for some reason made Pete hit Mr. Halbert – probably because he didn't feel comfortable hitting old Kilroy. Mr. Halbert doesn't believe in conflict – he was a conscientious objector during the Vietnam War – so he didn't hit Pete back. But he did pick up his bun filled with Sloppy Joe and threw it right at Pete's

> shirt. Nobody needs to know, but that was Pete's only shirt, and he had to go to work in one of my blouses for two days while I washed that shirt for him. Sloppy Joe really leaves a mark, you know – I'll have to cook something less colorful in the future. Anyway, when Kilroy saw what Mr. Halbert did, he got Mr. Halbert in a head lock, of course. That's when Mrs. Halbert came back from the bathroom. She has no problem with conflict, and, in fact, has a black belt in judo. She got Kilroy on the ground, bawling, while her husband tried to get his breath back. "Ma'am," Mr. Halbert said to me when he had finally come to, "I was real regretful to lose that Sloppy Joe, because you are one fine cook. But your dog Kilroy has no place at a dining table for humans."

Remember:

WORD CHOICE

- Synonyms
- Concrete in place of abstract
- Comparison
- Authenticating detail

Before you start rewriting the paragraph above, you may wish to read some examples of brilliantly vivid writing.

Michael Chabon, the author of *The Amazing Adventures of Kavalier & Clay*, a great novel about comic books, superheroes, and friendship, is a master of the well-turned sentence. Just look at this sentence from his novel *The Yiddish Policemen's Union*:

> Night is an orange smear over Sitka, a compound of fog and the light of sodium-vapor streetlamps. It has the translucence of onions cooked in chicken fat... Landsman can smell fish offal from the canneries, grease from the fry pits at Pearl of Manila, the spew of taxis, an intoxicating bouquet of fresh hat from Grinspoon's felting two blocks away.[1]

Imagine if, instead, the line said: "Night over Sitka has shades of orange, foggy and translucent. Landsman can smell fish, grease, taxi exhaust, and even the hat-felting shop."

1 Michael Chabon, *The Yiddish Policemen's Union*. New York: HarperCollins, 2007, p. 13.

Which version of the sentence puts you there more effectively? Some prefer the plainness of the second because it leaves the details to the reader to imagine. All the same, I really appreciate the vividness, immediacy, and imagination of the original example. It *really* puts me in the scene.

Now it's time for you to rewrite. Proceed piecemeal: Take the first couple of sentences and stare at them for a while:

> I wish Kilroy had better manners at the table. He eats so impolitely.

Think to yourself: Is there a way to say any of this more vividly? Can you be more specific about "better manners" the way I made "the weather was bad in Heathertown" more concrete? "Better manners" is pretty abstract when you think about it. "Better manners" how? What does Kilroy do now? You might say "I wish Kilroy didn't clear his nose at the table." Or "I wish Kilroy didn't slap his fellow diners." And guess what? We won't have our lesson on concision for some weeks, but here's an intro: Having such a vivid first sentence frees you from having to use a second one to clarify the point. "He eats so impolitely" can go.

CHALLENGE EXERCISES

1. Write your own two versions of a 300-word paragraph, the first simple, the second more vivid and original. Learning how to write an un-vivid paragraph is just as useful as practicing how to write a vivid one. It'll help you determine what kind of writer you are. I don't think Michael Chabon could write a plain sentence if he tried. Ernest Hemingway, on the other hand, couldn't do the opposite—his sentences read a lot more like my original piece about Kilroy: Simple, economical, precise. (We'll talk more about ways of speaking later this year, but you'll agree that even though the narrator speaks plainly in the original segment, she sounds fairly natural and believable. She's just a different character from the one in your revision, who speaks more elaborately.)

2. Find a long paragraph in the newspaper and rewrite it more vividly and originally.

3. Find a really well-written paragraph in a fiction book (such as the one above by Michael Chabon or one of your own choosing) and rewrite it more plainly.

FICTION • SECTION 3

PRECISION

WEEKS 8-10

LET'S GET TECHNICAL

Purpose: To further our understanding of specialized vocabulary and word choice (and learn something about research in the process).

Compare these two sentences:

> I moved the seat forward.
>
> I walked to the truck and levered the seat forward to usher Stephen into the club cab's rear compartment.[2]

What's different about these sentences? (A club cab is a kind of extension on the main seating area of a pickup truck.) Well, we'll agree that the second one is much more *precise*. Some things have only one name (unlike a "ball" —which might also be a "sphere," or, depending on the context, a "circle," or what have you—a "lever" can only be a "lever"), and anything but that name feels like a weak description of the item in question. It's as specific and precise as can be—like last week's "chicken bone," for example. You can't improve on it.

As we've discussed, the reader depends on a specific description in order to form an image of what's happening on the page. In the first instance, we're not quite sure what to imagine. "Seat" could be referring to anything—a seat on a train, a bus, a dental chair. "Moved" can mean a dozen things. But "levered" immediately gets us imagining that little automatic thingamajig (about the only substitute for "lever" I can

2 Wells Tower, "Retreat," in *Everything Ravaged, Everything Burned*. New York: Farrar, Straus and Giroux, 2010, p. 42.

think of) on the side of the seat that moves it forward. In the second sentence, there's no question that we're talking about a pick-up truck – one of those with a front cab and a rear cab. ("Rear cab" is another precise this-and-only-this term.) The second sentence uses **technical language**.

Good writers get as knowledgeable as possible about the specific community or lifestyle they're describing, so they can be as specific as possible in their descriptions for the reader. If a writer is describing the life of a car mechanic, he might want to figure out what a carburetor is, because his mechanic would know and might need to refer to it. If you're focusing on a fisherman, you need to know the difference between a bow and a stern. If you've ever heard of Method acting – where an actress preparing for a role starts acting, in real life, like the character she intends to portray – this would be the equivalent in writing. You don't have to start fixing cars for a living, but you'll get much closer to it than before if you decided to write a story about a car mechanic.

Your job this week will be to **pick a specialized line of work—dentist, motorcycle rider, gardener, teacher—and write a 500-word scene from this person's life, using technical language.**

An aside about two important things: subcultures and research.

You will need to **research** the line of work you choose. This research will inevitably take you far beyond the mere knowledge of technical terms that members of **subcultures** use (**subcultures** are specific communities that have their own rules and vocabulary). There's no way to engage in language research without doing character research. What do fly fishermen worry about? What do tobacco farmers worry about? Cardiologists? If you are writing about a character in a specialized line of work or lifestyle, you can't do a very good job of imagining the world *through that character's eyes* if you don't know the first thing about rock collecting, car mechanics, dentistry, or farming. You need to be able to inhabit that character's profession or obsession effectively. Besides, you may find it tough to arrive at a story idea without finding out more about what that person does.

For instance, I've always been interested in people who look after ancestral graves for Russian or Indian or Japanese families who've emigrated to other countries, and rarely return home. I don't know *what* it is about this line of work that intrigues me, and I certainly don't have a story idea related to it. That's because I've never looked into it closely. But by doing a little research, I can learn enough concrete detail about the lives of the individuals involved to get steered toward a story idea.

Your research may even go beyond both terminology and character. Often, certain professions—whitewater-rafting guide, for instance—have a lot to do with landscape and setting. The language of the profession is the language of the place. It's also the language of the way people speak (dialect), which will be the focus of next week's lesson.

I should mention that there's a proud tradition in fiction of authors writing with a purposeful ignorance about specialized lines of work or locales, such as Saul Bellow's novel *Henderson the Rain King*, which centers on life in an African village even though Bellow had never visited Africa. There is a value to this kind of writing as well, and it's really important to understand that too much research can suffocate a piece of writing and make it sound like a textbook instead of a drama. However, you have to learn how to research before you can decide to do without it.

To give you an example before I send you off on your assignment, I just wrote a short story that concerns a rancher in North Dakota. With winter approaching, he has to wrap his trees in burlap, to protect them from the frost. What kind of trees do they have in North Dakota, I wondered. I did a little research online, but not finding anything definitive, I called the North Dakota Tree Information Center at North Dakota State University. A friendly gentleman agreed to spend a couple of minutes on the phone and told me all sorts of fascinating things, like the fact that the sun is what hurts North Dakota trees in the winter, not the cold, because there are no leaves to obstruct its brutal shine. I also made an interesting new acquaintance, whom I promised to get back to if my story ever got published.

So what is your assignment? It has two parts.

First, do a little research on a lifestyle or profession that you don't know much about. If you're stuck, pick a character in your hometown with a specific activity. If you live by the water, maybe you'll pick a fisherman. If you live by an auto plant, perhaps you'll pick an engineer. Then, using the Internet (Wikipedia, which isn't always reliable, is actually great for research projects like this because you're only looking for a general idea of how things work in a given field) or the library, try to find out as much as you can about that person's activity.

Don't stop with the Internet or the library. If your family knows someone involved in this kind of technical profession, ask to interview this person, by phone or live. If your mom manages a furniture store, go in and look at the models, paying special attention to the language used to describe the options. If your dad is a mechanic, ask to come to work with him so you can figure out what a timing belt is. Obsessions work just as well as professions: If your sister loves fashion, spend some time with her figuring out the difference between ponte-knit and palazzo pants.

Don't make your life difficult by trying to describe a mercenary soldier in North Africa. If you have a specialist easily accessible to you, talk to that person. A well-rendered grocery clerk is a far greater fictional achievement than a poorly-rendered astronaut. On the other hand, if you know everything there is to know about medieval princes, feel free to focus on a medieval prince instead of the local dentist.

Now, we have to set some limits on this research because you could be doing it for a year if you wanted to. A writer needs to find out enough to be able to imagine life as that character, but not so much that he gets distracted from his main mission, which is to write a good story. If every other word in your scene is some kind of complicated technical term, that's going to draw your reader's attention away from the story. It's going to be a pretty boring, wooden story if our dentist uses his dialogue to say things like, "Mandy, could you please give me the scapular drill so I can file the molar in spot #31 for our client Richard Moss?" Mandy already knows what a scapular drill is (by the way, that term is made up, at least as far as dental equipment goes), and the dentist doesn't have to tell Mandy what he's doing with Mr. Moss. Likely the dentist would just say something like: "Mandy – scap drill, please."

Which is why, when your research is finished—when, let's say, you've collected 2-3 pages of information or about 400–600 words—read it over and set it aside. Your mission isn't to include as much of it as possible in the story. Your mission is to have it *inform* your understanding of the character and his field. This material will seep into your brain and snake its way down to your short story *even without you making a conscious effort to include detail x and detail y.* Trust me on this. Do the research and set it aside for a day.

Second, write a 500-word scene, showing a character in your chosen profession or lifestyle. Don't revisit your research too closely after you've started writing, unless you need a specific term. Just let it float around back there.

Since the focus here is word choice, don't worry about infusing the scene with too many elements of a plotted story, such as conflict, quest, suspense, etc. Just give us a character in his or her element.

So, to recap:

1. Choose a profession or hobby or specialization to focus on.

2. Spend some time at the library or on the Internet or first-hand learning about the profession. You're not looking for anything in particular. Just let your curiosity guide you.

3. Settle on an aspect of the specialist's life that intrigues you. Try to think of a situation that incorporates this interest. If you get fascinated—or horrified—by how early fishermen rise, that could be your focus: An old fisherman is bumbling around his house in the dark, trying not to wake up his wife, as he gets ready for a long day of fishing.

4. Start bringing the scene to life. Maybe say some random phrases in the voice of the specialist. Is there anyone else in the scene? What are they like? What's the setting? Remember the 5 Essentials and flesh each out before starting the scene.

Remember, your final scene should be around 500 words long.

CHALLENGE EXERCISES

1. Go further. Write a scene that's more of an actual part of a story than the above kind of fragment. Come up with a situation somehow related to the particulars of the main character's subculture—the rock collectors of southeast Texas are having a congress; the person whose collection is judged the best will go on to a national tournament; and someone has just swiped Seth Cronenberg's collection from the trunk of his car—and take us through a scene in which this plot somehow gets revealed. (Your specialized language here may have to do with rock collecting, but also the unique landscape of southeast Texas.)

2. Sensitize yourself as a reader to technical language. Go to the library and read a specialized magazine or journal for a half-hour, such as *Popular Science* or *Car and Driver*. Pick up a book on a specialized subject—Bernard Malamud's *The Natural* is about baseball, Tim O'Brien's *The Things They Carried* is about war—and write out in your notebook, as you read the opening 10-15 pages, every word that could be construed as "technical."

3. Preview next week's exercise on dialect by picking up books that feature regional speech–Sherwood Anderson's *Winesburg, Ohio*, Richard Wright's *Native Son*, and so on–and doing the same for non-standard language.

DIALECT

Purpose: To practice precision in word choice by learning about dialect—the special speech patterns of people in different places and periods of time.

Last week, you learned about technical vocabulary. This week, you're going to learn about technical dialogue. If every character in your story sounds the same—even though one is a fisherman from Massachusetts, another an immigrant from the Soviet Union, and a third of West Indian descent—that's not very believable, is it?

Dialect has to do with the different way people speak in different places, cultures, and ages. This goes beyond the different way people pronounce the same words. (A New Yorker will say "arts." Someone from Cape Cod will say "ahts.") It also has to do with word choice, syntax, and phrases chosen.

If you've seen American writing from the 18th century, you probably know that it's more formal and arch than the way we speak today. Here's an entry from the diary of the great statesman John Adams:

> There is no greater mortification than to sit with a half-dozen Witts, deliberating upon a Petition, Address, or Memorial. These great Witts, these subtle Criticks, these refined Genius's, these learned Lawyers, these

> wise Statesmen, are so fond of shewing their Parts and Powers, as to make their Consultations very tedius.[3]

Doesn't that sound stiff and formal? Someone making the same point today would probably say, "These guys are pretty full of themselves, aren't they?"

In the same way, if you've ever seen an old Western, surely you've heard characters "fixin'" to do one thing or another (as opposed to be "about to be") and "reckon" this or that (as opposed to "think" it).

Take a look at this brief excerpt from Zadie Smith's novel *Autograph Man*, in which a young man tries to purchase a subway ticket from a "gray-haired woman sitting behind a pane of glass":

> "Can I get one from Mountjoy, please." ...
> "You waan what? You goin' Mountjoy?"
> "No -- no, I just *came* --"
> "Bwoy -- speak into de ting; me kyan hear you."
> "I said, I just *came* from Mountjoy --"
> "So you want a ticket back dare?"
> "No, I -- just -- the machine at Mount -- There was a train coming, so I just jumped --"
> ... "So, what you are sayin' -- and feel free to correct me if I am perchance mistaken -- is dat you skipped de fare; you jus' skip it like it *nutting* --"[4]

This is a brilliant rendering of speech from the Caribbean. You can tell the author has listened very, very closely, running the words over and over in her mind until she arrived at the perfect mangled renderings of them. These "mangled" words – kyan, waan, de ting – form a beautiful new language, and serve as a reminder that language isn't fixed, that words can be molded just like dough, that there's nothing sacred about them as they are.

3 John Adams, *The Diary and Autobiography of John Adams*, L. H. Butterfield ed. Cambridge, MA: Belknap Press, 1961, pp. 156-57.

4 Zadie Smith, *The Autograph Man*. New York: Random House, 2002, p. 73.

Your assignment this week will be to transcribe some dialect, just as Zadie Smith has done. Let's use her excerpt as a guideline: It features **100 words and eight lines of dialogue**, so your job will be to come up with the same.

You'll probably want to use a tape recorder to capture the dialect that you'll transcribe. Feel free to condense, edit, and change the words around so that they make sense, but be sure to write down the exact words that your subjects use.

Also, feel free to spell the words you hear any way that you'd like, just as Zadie Smith has done. For this exercise, "correct" spelling goes out the window. Listen to the *sound* of the speech and try to render that as precisely as you can. By the way, this will come in very handy in your poetry section.

> As mentioned above, misspelling is only one way to render dialect. Word choice and syntax are two others, and as you'll learn in the future, they're far more effective than misspelling in suggesting regional speech. (But it's fun to misspell words for a week, and it can certainly work to great effect, as it does in Zadie Smith's novel.) Americans say "apartment" and "elevator"; the British say "flat" and "lift." A New Orleanian might add "sugar" at the end of a sentence as a term of endearment, as in this excerpt from John Kennedy Toole's *A Confederacy of Dunces* (It features a misspelling, too):

> I know what it is, sugar... The anonymous letters my poppa useta get... Vicious.[5]

Or take this story, by William Faulkner in an interview with the literary magazine *The Paris Review.* Pay attention to the bolded words/phrases:

> My Great-Grandfather Murry was a kind and gentle man, to us children

5 John Kennedy Toole, *A Confederacy of Dunces* . Baton Rouge, LA: LSU Press, 1980, p. 174.

> anyway. That is, although he was a Scot, he was to us neither especially pious nor stern either: he was simply a man of inflexible principles. One of them was everybody, children on up through all adults present, had to have a verse from the Bible **ready and glib at tongue-tip** when we gathered at the table for breakfast each morning. If you didn't have your scripture verse ready, you didn't have any breakfast; you would be excused long enough to leave the room and **swot** one up. There was a maiden aunt, a kind of sergeant major for this duty, who retired with the culprit and gave him a brisk **breezing** which **carried him over the jump** next time.[6]

The bolded words and phrases are distinctive to Faulkner's upbringing; his vocabulary is part of his dialect.

Same goes for syntax. Residents of different parts of a country will certainly organize their sentences differently, speaking declaratively or in terms of questions, putting nouns before verbs or after, and repeating certain words for emphasis or not.

Now, set out to find your dialect.

Where? You might follow a writer's first and most important guidance: Look around. Where do you live? Virginians speak differently from Mississippians, Alaskans, and Montanans. Go to the grocery store; turn on the local TV station; listen closely to a neighbor. The geographical variety of the United States presents lots of rich opportunities to learn about dialect.

If you can't find subjects to record and transcribe, go online. Find audio clips on YouTube from other regions of your country, or go to the BBC website for news videos in British English, or the website of an Australian newspaper.

Much of your language-arts instruction has been about learning how to say something correctly. That is important. *Very* important. (You have to learn the rules before you can break them.) But there's no disputing the fact that most of what we hear every

6 William Faulkner, "The Art of Fiction," in *The Paris Review Interviews*, Vol. II. New York: Picador, 2007, p. 51.

day is nonstandard speech, and, sometimes, the technically incorrect usage becomes a language of its own, a language that powerfully conjures a specific time, place, or people. And who's to say then that's "incorrect"? The job of creative writing isn't to wag a disciplinary finger at the mistakes of the world. It's to capture the world around us in its full, complicated, and sometimes improper glory. Capturing the way people *really* speak is a central part of that.

CHALLENGE EXERCISES

This week's assignment limits you to places where English is spoken, but so many places fit that category, and in all of them English is spoken differently. For a challenge, you might:

1. Render the same dialogue in two different dialects. This would require you, in the second case, to use your imagination. Let's say you've transcribed a part of a speech by a politician from the BBC website, and you would like to render the same dialogue with a Caribbean accent. Since no example of that exists, you'll have to imagine how the BBC politician might sound if he was from the Caribbean. For this, you'll need to spend some time listening to Caribbean speech, in general, to get the hang of how it sounds.

2. For an even bigger challenge, write both pieces of dialogue from scratch, after getting a good feel for some dialect.

CONCISION

Purpose: To learn how to write more efficiently and powerfully.

One of writing's most important lessons has been articulated by writers as diverse as Thomas Jefferson and Friedrich Nietzsche: "This letter would have been shorter if I'd had more time." That is, more time would have given, say, Jefferson, an opportunity to go over what he had written and cut out unnecessary words. Why is this important? We take a lot more pleasure in writing that is tight rather than flabby. Flabby writing, like a flabby person, moves slowly, laboriously. Tight writing sprints along, and the reader sprints along with it.

Let me give you an example from the author Bill Bryson's wonderful book *Bill Bryson's Dictionary of Troublesome Words*: The phrase "thinking to oneself." In a sentence from a story, this would sound something like "Will Straw was thinking to himself that it was time to wrap his trees in burlap when Jack Robinson walked into the store."

As Bryson explains, would we not make absolutely the same point if we simply got rid of "to himself"? If we're thinking, by definition, are we not thinking "to ourselves"? If I saw a sentence like that in a story, I'd get out my pencil and cross the words "to himself" right out in a silent rebuke to the author. (I also wouldn't think much of his reference to "trees." As we all know from our lessons on concreteness and specificity, the reader's imagination will come alive far more effectively if the author tells us what *kind* of trees Will Straw has. Think back to my story about those North Dakota trees.)

Here's an example that comes from the mystery writer Raymond Chandler:

> She came over *near me* and smiled *with her mouth* and she had little sharp predatory teeth.
>
> He walked slowly *across the floor* towards us.[7]

Any idea what's wrong with these sentences? You have a hint in the italicized portions. They spell out things that we would have assumed just fine without them. If someone comes over, then they're near you. If they're smiling, they're definitely not doing it with their knees! And unless we're in space, these characters are definitely walking across a floor.

Here's another example, this one invented, followed by a tighter version of the same sentence. Can you see the difference?

> *We* made *advance* reservations for *12* noon, my *fellow* classmates and I, eager to meet *together* again and renew a *common* bond which dates *back* to when we were *young* lads. (31 words)
>
> My classmates and I made reservations for noon, eager to meet and renew a bond from youth. (17 words)

This week, we will practice concision.

In Level 1, I asked you to transform bloated sentences into tighter ones. This week, you're going to do it with whole paragraphs, which will challenge you to consolidate by borrowing information from other sentences or leaving it until later. Think of the Week 7 scene

7 Raymond Chandler, *The Big Sleep*. New York: Alfred Knopf, 1939, pp. 5-6.

involving Kilroy, the quarrelsome hound. The two opening sentences—"I wish Kilroy had better manners at the table. He eats so impolitely."—say essentially the same thing, easily becoming the more economical "I wish Kilroy wasn't such a shame at the table."

We will start together. I will provide you with an excerpt from the start of a story I invented for this exercise. I'll condense the first paragraph so you can see how it's done and why. Then you'll try yourself with the second one. Here's the two-paragraph excerpt:

> The cold winter came in without advance warning. One day, it was seventy degrees, and the next the temperature dropped all the way down to thirty. Snowflakes appeared from the sky within hours. I was caught completely unaware. The jacket I had hanging up in the closet wasn't worth all that much, if thirty degrees is what we were dealing with on the thermometer. I picked up the telephone and called my son Rich. I said, "Rich, come and get me in your car, we have to drive down to the box store and stock me up for the winter."
>
> I need my son Rich to drive me because my eyes can't see things too well anymore. My son Rich isn't too easy on the go himself. If I'm blind, he's fat. Barely fits, that bulky frame of his, behind the wheel of his car. He's my son, so I love him no matter what. And last time I checked, Wal-Mart doesn't deliver warm coats, and I need one really bad because of this weather. So I call Rich, and when I hang up I move to the bay windows in the living room, so I can hear him when he comes up on the steps and rings the bell. Because the thing is – I can't hear too well, either.

Below find my edit of the first paragraph. Have a look and then read my explanation underneath.

> The winter came without warning. In one day, the temperature dropped forty degrees and it started to snow. My jacket wasn't worth much, so I called Rich: "Son, we have to drive down to the box store."

37 words versus the original's 100. If we're thinking of words as dollars, I saved 63!

How did I do this? I asked myself: What information is repetitive? What information is, perhaps, not repetitive, but could be presented in fewer words without the whole thing sounding as clipped as an instruction manual? What information is obvious without it having to be spelled out?

Do we know winters are cold without the author having to tell us? We sure do. "Came in" is just a longer way of saying "came."

(I do want to pause here, however, to note that this character has a particular "voice" – or dialect, if you will. We will learn more about voice next year, but all you need to understand about it for now is that we have here an older character who speaks in a folksy way that isn't overly concerned with directness and the most economical use of language. So even as we cut unnecessary words, we have to remain ready to leave some in if they strike us as particularly expressive of his "style" of speaking.")

To finish up with the first sentence, however, there can be no argument that all warnings are "advance" by nature.

Look at the next two sentences: I combined them, finding a way to convey all the same information using fewer words. In the following sentence, you might argue that "completely unawares" should have stayed because it's the man's "voice," instead of being folded into the following sentence about not having proper winter clothes (which implies being caught unawares by the weather). And that would be a fine argument.

I cut "hanging up in the closet" because we can assume that about a jacket. And even if this jacket isn't hanging up in the closet, so what? Its exact location isn't of great importance to the story. "Wasn't worth much" is the same as "wasn't worth all that much" and the remainder of that sentence – "if thirty degrees...." -- is information already known to us.

"I picked up the telephone" is unnecessary because how else can one call someone else? Maybe by cell phone, but this is a bit like the location of the jacket – it isn't very material to the story. I also changed "my son Rich" to "Rich," but then inserted "Son" when the old man speaks, so it's clear who Rich is (but using one less word). If this seems overly fussy to you, think of each word you use in a story as a dollar. I don't know about you but I'd rather spend three dollars instead of four.

As for the last sentence, can you guess why I cut what I did?

Let's move to the second paragraph. **Rewrite the paragraph in as few words as you can.**

As you do, ask yourself questions:

1. Is there information that's repetitive?
2. Is there information that is obvious without having to be spelled out?
3. Is there information whose spelling out isn't that important to the focus of the story?
4. Is there a way to say the same thing in fewer words? (Let's remember Thomas Jefferson!)

This is enough to keep in mind without having to worry about making exceptions for those repetitions and verbosities that give this character his distinctly folksy brand of speech, so don't worry about preserving that unless you feel like it. And you'll notice that my rewrite was quite dry, as far as vivid writing goes. Don't worry about rewriting in rich, memorable ways. For now, just focus on saying the same things more concisely.

When you're finished, you can compare your rewrite with mine, in the mentor section. Who managed to cut more words? Either way, decide what you'd buy if you had the saved money in hand.

CHALLENGE EXERCISES

1. Rewrite the above two paragraphs not only concisely, but in vivid, original language, the way you did in Week 7.

2. Preview next year's lessons on voice—and refresh your recollection of dialect—by infusing your rewrite with as much distinctive speech by the older man as possible. You don't have to keep my "folksy" style; you can invent one of your own. You might spend some time listening to someone you know as a model. If this changes what exactly the old man is saying, or who he is, that's fine.

FICTION • SECTION 4

SHOW AND TELL

WEEKS 11-13

SHOW AND TELL

Purpose: To better understand the distinction between showing and telling in storytelling.

To prepare yourself for this lesson, look back at Weeks 1 and 2. Those lessons provide you with a great primer on showing and telling.

To review:

A writer has to make certain things clear to the reader. For instance, he's writing a story about a young woman named Jane, who, in an early scene, doesn't help an old lady cross the crosswalk. Why? Is it because Jane's not very nice, or because she doesn't see the old lady, or because Jane is weighed down with bags, or because she doesn't want to be patronizing to the old lady, or because the old lady is notorious for refusing help? Any of these is possible. The author probably knows the answer, and needs to convey it to the reader, so the reader has the necessary information to decide what he thinks about Jane.

Let's say the reason is that Jane isn't very nice. As discussed in Weeks 1 and 2, the fastest way to indicate that is to **show** Jane doing something unkind or **tell** the reader the information straight out:

> **Tell**: Jane was ornery.
> **Show**: Jane watched the old woman drag herself across the crosswalk as the light started to blink red, then started tapping away on her phone.

You could do the same with any of the other possibilities above:
Because she doesn't see the old lady:

> **Tell**: Jane didn't help because didn't see the old lady.
> **Show**: As the old woman dragged herself across the crosswalk, Jane typed furiously on her cell phone.

Because she's weighed down with bags.

> **Tell**: Jane didn't help because was weighed down with bags.
> **Show**: Jane stared helplessly, her hands weighed down with grocery bags, as an old woman dragged herself across the street.

Because the old lady refuses the help:

> **Tell**: Jane didn't help because the old woman was notorious for refusing it.
> **Show**: Jane tried to thread her arm through the old woman's, but the latter barked that she'd been crossing streets for 93 years on her own, and would keep it that way.

Other examples:

> **Tell**: Clyde Jenkins did not have his right leg.
> **Show**: Jenkins hopped on his one leg to fetch the grapefruit juice.
> **Tell**: The day was bright.
> **Show**: "What you doing, Mrs. T?"
> "Oh, I'm making sun tea, Charlie! In weather like this? This water'll be boiling before you know it!"

A teacher of mine called the "showing" in the 2nd example the Omelette Approach. That is, as in a folded omelette, the fact that the day is sunny and bright is "folded into," or implied by, the fact that Mrs. T is making sun tea. The conversation between the two characters is ostensibly about what Mrs. T is doing. But the author has managed to sneak in the information that the day is sunny and bright.

This week, we'll start by practicing converting telling into showing, as I did in the first three examples in this lesson. Below, I provide you with 10 "told" details. Your job is to convert them into 10 "shown" details.

Remember: You can show through a character's action ("she tore the doll in half"), thoughts ("her mind broke out in hives at the thought of spinach"), dress ("he grabbed the one shirt that didn't have holes"), speech ("I hate you!"), and so forth.

1. Stanley was lazy.
2. Beverly was pretty.
3. The weather had turned bad.
4. They had never met.
5. Overcast skies always made him depressed.
6. John couldn't eat fruit.
7. In this community, no secret stayed that way for long.
8. Randy Brown had a big ranch.
9. He was a pacifist.
10. The trees had been planted by his grandfather.

How might you do the first one? Start by figuring out your options. How can you show that Stanley is lazy? You can do it through action, appearance, speech. You can show Stanley clicking through TV channels while surrounded by pizza boxes and dirty laundry. Or you can show him telling his roommate that he'll fix the leak in the roof tomorrow, and his roommate can respond that Stanley's been saying that for three weeks.

CHALLENGE EXERCISE

1. Pick up your favorite book and re-read several pages. Mark every instance of telling (T) and every instance of showing (S).

2. Copy out a page of the book and rewrite every instance of telling as showing, and vice versa.

SHOW AND TELL

Purpose: To continue examining the differences and similarities between showing and telling.

This week, we're going to continue with our *show and tell* practice. Last week, you practiced turning "told" details into "shown" details. This week, you're going to practice integrating both kinds of telling into the opening 300 words of a short story. Below, find several situations, the first of which I'll use to give you an example.

Situation 1:
A young man refuses to get out of bed – for breakfast, for his schoolwork, even to go out on a date. His family is mystified, then angry, then scared. They try various tricks to get him out of bed.

Situation 2:
A man who is sick of living in a city embarks on a trip to remote parts of the American West or the Australian interior. In an isolated mountain pass, after not seeing a soul for hours, a bright day suddenly turns rainy and then snowy, In the gathering storm, the man accidentally runs over another man who is crossing the road.

Situation 3:
An illegal immigrant in New York learns that his brother, an illegal immigrant in California, has died under mysterious circumstances. Since he doesn't have a driver's license, he can't fly, so he gets hold of a car (tell us how) and goes that way, hoping he won't get stopped by the police.

Here's my stab at Situation 1.

It was twenty minutes past the hour when Trevor usually got up when Mrs. Sanderson wondered why he wasn't at the breakfast table along with the other children. She had heard the alarm go off in his bedroom, and she had heard it turned off. His oatmeal was on the kitchen table, getting cold. The other children chattered among themselves.

Mrs. Sanderson put down her magazine and walked the carpet to Trevor's bedroom, feeling a lurch in her stomach. "Honey?" she called, knocking on the door and gently pushing it open.

Trevor was awake. He was brushing his teeth. In bed. Next to him, on a shelf where he usually kept the books he read before falling asleep, there were three cups: One for the toothbrush, one filled with water, and one that he filled with the toothpaste water in his mouth. It was as if he had set them up the night before. He placed his tooth brush in the first cup, took a gulp from the second, rinsed quickly, and dumped it in the third.

"Hiya, mom," he said.

"Um, honey?" Mrs. Sanderson said. "What's going on?"

"I'm brushing my teeth," Trevor said. "What's it look like?"

"But there's a bathroom for that!" Mrs. Sanderson exclaimed. "Why aren't you at breakfast?"

"Because I'm here," Trevor said. "I'm not going to get out of bed today."

"Why not?!" Mrs. Sanderson exclaimed in horror.

Trevor gave this some thought, feeling the bristles of his toothbrush with his thumb. "I don't know," he said finally.

"Trevor, you quit this right now. Up, up, up!" Mrs. Sanderson said and rushed at her son's bed.

Notice that I never explained what was going on, for example: "Trevor refused to get out of bed." This information didn't even appear in the opening until 2/3 of the way through. I described—I showed—what was happening through physical description: the house, the hour, the kitchen, the morning rituals (alarm clock, breakfast), the boy inexplicably still in bed. There's a fair amount of telling, too—see the first paragraph—but it's the kind of telling that *describes what's going on* instead of *explains what things mean.*

Your turn. **Choose one of the other two situations above, or invent one of your own, and write 300 words about it, telling or showing us all the critical details.** It may help you to start by not worrying about show-and-tell. Don't even think about it. Just try to expand the thumbnails into something that "feels" like a story. Once you're at 300 words or so, back up and go over what you've written, thinking of ways to expand telling into showing, and vice versa. If you go over your limit, don't worry about it.

CHALLENGE EXERCISES

1. To understand the problem with pure showing, write a 500-word segment in which nothing is told. See if that's even feasible.

2. Flip the challenge and write a 500-word segment (it could even be the same one) in which nothing is shown. See how much less vivid the result is?

AUTHENTICATING DETAIL

Purpose: To practice coming up with that telling detail that convinces the reader he's really there.

One of the most effective ways of showing is through something called **authenticating detail.** What is that? It's not extremely different from converting abstractions into concrete details, but it's worth highlighting and practicing on its own.

Compare these two sentences:

> "There was a vase on the tablecloth," You can imagine that, right? You know what a vase is and you know what a tablecloth is. Now take the following sentence:
>
> "The lace tablecloth had scuffed edges and on it stood a plastic vase bearing a crumpled carnation." That would be a lot more vivid and effective, wouldn't it? Those extra details put you there in a different way.

By the way, note the metaphorical use of "crumpled," which usually applies to paper. Obviously this isn't literal—the carnation isn't crumpled—but that's the way it *looks*. The metaphor captures the feeling rather than the fact. Note also the way I've managed to convey that this table probably stands in a home of modest means, if the tablecloth edges are scuffed and the carnation is crumpled. And yet this is a home that at least aspires, or aspired once, to a measure of homeyness. At least there is a tablecloth and carnation at all. See how much you can convey through showing without ever having to say "It was a home of modest means whose owner tried to add festive touches all the same"?

Let me give you a different example, by the Colombian novelist Gabriel García Márquez:

> If you say that there are elephants flying in the sky, people are not going to believe you. But if you say that there are four hundred and twenty-five elephants flying in the sky, people will probably believe you.[8]

The "four hundred and twenty-five" is the authenticating detail. It's that little bit of very particular information that makes you think, "Well, that must have really happened then."

This is why describing from observation is often more effective than describing from memory. In our memory, soccer fields are perfect, green rectangles with two nets and painted lines. On closer inspection of a real field, however, we might see that one of the nets is ripped, the grass has a bluish tint from the quality of the light, and there's a funny squiggle in one of the penalty-box lines. Those are the authenticating details that put the reader there, in that particular soccer field at that particular moment – rather than in some generic, one-size-fits-all soccer field that clearly has been dreamed up by an author writing a Story. (Of course, that's what's happening, but the writer's trick is to make the reader forget that, to help her fall into the story and forget she's reading.)

A side note: Authentic details are often unexpected and nonstandard. As human beings, we like to impose order on our observations; we filter out inconsistencies so things make sense. But the world remains a strange, surprising place:

- Someone I know, a responsible family man who works in a quiet job, is, in his private time, obsessed with cooking the perfect shish-kebab, and spends his weekends at the grill, perfecting and perfecting.
- The sign in a store window that says "Restrooms for customers only" while another says "Restrooms 50c."
- A restaurant menu that offers every kind of sandwich except chicken salad.

These kinds of "oddities" and "contradictions" may more accurately be called the norm: They're everywhere. And, counter-intuitively, they evoke a feeling of authenticity far better than tablecloths that look like all other tablecloths and restaurants that serve a full menu.

8 From "Gabriel García Márquez, The Art of Fiction No. 69." *The Paris Review*, Issue 82, Winter 1981.

This is something that even advanced writers forget. When we write, we create a world from scratch, and when we do, we often forget to make it imperfect and non-linear. Like the real world.

This is the reason for research, too. If I'm writing a story that involves someone who's been run over by a car, and I don't know what happens to a leg after a car runs into it, I'm only going to be able to make broad references to bone, blood, etc. If I had done some research, I'd come into possession of all kinds of authenticating details, many of them hard to imagine out of thin air.

So, this week, you're going to practice coming up with authenticating details. Below find a list of generic entries. Your job is to **make these places, objects, characters, etc. come alive to us in descriptions (from a sentence to a paragraph long) that brim with authenticating detail,** which means that you'll need to come up with a character(s) in a situation as well. Let me give you an example from each of the categories below.

> 1. Table:
> Tory had decided she needed a table that expanded into twice the original size. In ten years, she hadn't expanded it once.

How odd: Tory insisted on a table that could be folded, retracted, expanded, but she hasn't done it once in ten years! This contradiction is the authenticating detail.

> 2. Judge:
> As the prosecutor began his summation, Judge Akin stared at the cufflinks of a man in the front row. Was that bone? It had to be. Judge Akin peered at his own —mere onyx—and frowned.

We tend to imagine judges as grave creatures, brows furrowed, listening to testimony and appeal. So we forget they're human beings with the same tendency to distraction, boredom, envy, and curiosity as all of us. This judge's focus on a man's cufflinks instead of the case at hand is the authenticating detail. Note that if the judge was merely bored by the prosecutor, that wouldn't be enough. It's the specificity of the cufflinks that does it. (Note also the "technical language": "summation," not something generic like "speech.")

3. Beach:

Charlie cut a toe on the rocks that dotted the shoreline. "All the weather this year scoured the sand right off the beach," his mom said, passing him antibiotic ointment.

Here, research provides the authenticating detail. When the water gets especially stormy, it scours sand off the beach, exposing the jagged rock that used to be buried and softened by the sand. Nothing is necessarily odd or inconsistent here. In this case, it's Charlie's mom's know-how that authenticates the sentence. Note as well that dialogue is a fine way of authenticating.

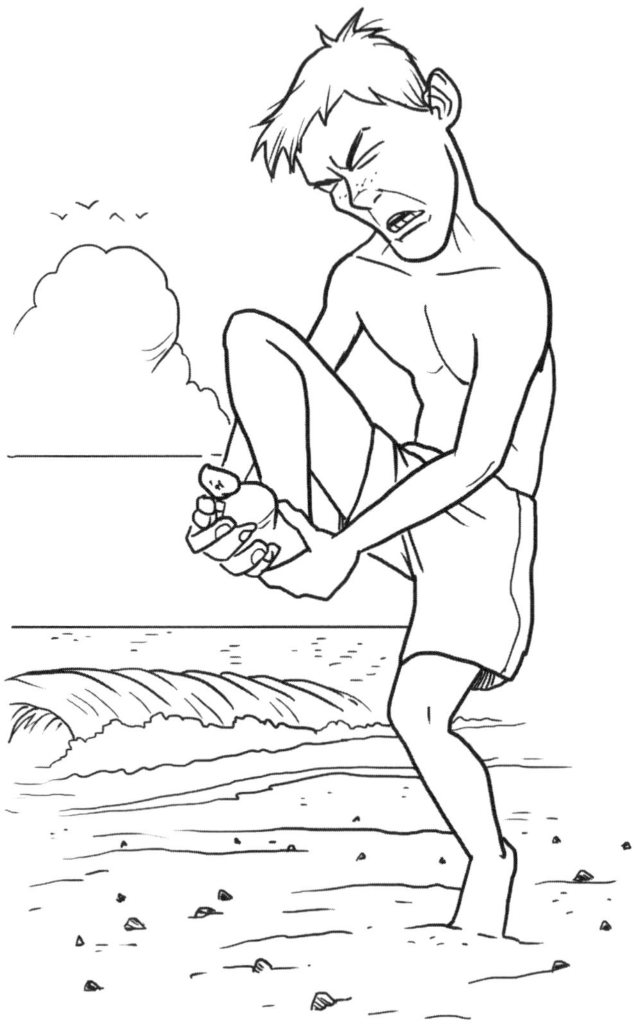

It's your turn. I've already done three of the below. **Do at least one more from each category.**

Objects:

- [ ] Table
- [ ] Jeans
- [ ] Hot-air balloon
- [ ] Telephone
- [ ] Ice-cream truck

Characters:

- [ ] Judge
- [ ] A woman named Christina
- [ ] Circus clown

- [ ] Pigeon
- [ ] Mom

Places:

- [ ] Beach
- [ ] Highway
- [ ] Basement
- [ ] Bandstand
- [ ] Bleachers

CHALLENGE EXERCISE

1. Find 10 authenticating details in a book you're currently reading. Remember: You're looking for:

   a. imperfection

   b. contradiction

   c. detail

   d. technical know-how

   e. anything that makes you forget you're reading fiction

FICTION • SECTION 5

GETTING AWAY FROM YOURSELF:

Point of view refresher and beyond

WEEKS 14-16

SO MANY POINTS OF VIEW

Purpose: To learn about a broader range of point of view.

In previous levels of this series, we discussed first- and third-person point of view. That is, first-person refers to stories that are told by an "I" character, whereas third-person refers to stories told by a narrator who's either off-stage or part of the action. And then there are narrators who know a lot about what's going on in the minds of other characters and those who don't.

We can organize our thoughts about point of view by asking three questions:

I. Who's telling the story?
II. How much does the narrator know?
III. To what extent is s/he a part of the story?

This week, we'll add a fourth question:

IV. To whom is this person telling the story?

Let's take these questions one by one.

I. Who's telling the story?

a. first-person ("I") and

b. third-person ("he" or "she") narrators. Some stories have

c. second-person narration ("you"). Here's an example: "You wake at dawn and watch the sky go from bronze to silver to gold, like an Olympic pedestal. You slip into a swimsuit still damp from last night's practice. Two practices a day, the first one before full light. You wouldn't trade it for anything, the cold water like a shock."

That is, instead of talking about oneself ("I go to swimming practice") or another character ("He goes to swimming practice"), the narrator is talking to someone, describing his actions *to* him. I know it sounds a bit strange, but it's just another way of telling the story.

d. There are also, more rarely, **collective narrators**, that is, those who tell the story from the perspective of a group.

We don't condone that kind of behavior in this town. We are a law-abiding community. You can't get things like that by us, no, sir. When we welcome you, we welcome you, but when you don't respond with grace, we'll run you right out.

So, to recap, we have four kinds of narration:

- I
- You
- He/She/They
- We (plural first person)

The first and third are the most common.

Let's move on to the next question in our classification system:

II. How much does the narrator know about what's going on for the other characters?

a. Some narrators know everything about the story, even a character's private thoughts. They're known as *omniscient*, although the exact terminology isn't that important. A first-person narrator, by virtue of being a part of the story, is limited by what anyone in the real world is limited by: we can understand only so much about why other people are the way they are. A third-person narrator, on the other hand, can participate in a kind of illusion: He or she knows everything about what's inside the characters' minds.

Just pick up any short story or novel you love and pay special attention to who's telling the story and how much he or she seems to understand about the other characters.

b. Sometimes, a third-person narrator will stick close to a single character's point of view. The technical term is *close third-person point of view*, but the terms are not our greatest concern right now. For instance, in an earlier draft of the novel I'm working on, the story was told by some unnamed, off-stage narrator who could infiltrate many characters' thoughts. But this narrator tended to see things the way the main character, a journalist named Slava Gelman, did. So if Slava thought something was strange, the narrator did, too. In this way, he was close to Slava (close third-person narration.) Here's an example:

> He stared at her as she punched the buttons on the phone. Was she angry, or did she simply do everything to make a point?

A narrator who can get inside his characters' heads would answer this question, or not have to ask it in the first place, writing instead something like "She punched the buttons of the phone with the emphasis with which she did everything."

Basically, this concept refers to how much the narrator can make clear to us about what's going on the story.

c. There is a third kind of narrator (called an *objective* narrator) who explains nothing, either because he doesn't know or because he won't tell. This kind of narrator would say:

> She punched the buttons of the phone.

We are left to guess – and extrapolate from other parts of the story – why this person is punching the keypad of the phone. If it seems like objective telling sounds like pure showing, I'd say that's a very astute observation.

III. The next question in our classification is: To what extent is the narrator a part of the story?

This is a quick one to answer. First-person narrators more or less have to be part of the story, even if a tangential one. Think about it: How can an "I" tell a story that he isn't part of, or witness to? If you can find a book or short story that features an "I" narrator who has absolutely no relationship to the story, then you're off the hook for this lesson's exercise.

Third-person narrators can be entirely off-stage, some mysterious being who's relaying all the details.

And finally:

IV. To whom is the narrator telling the story?

In her wise and useful textbook *Writing Fiction*, Janet Burroway points out that stories tend to address three kinds of audiences: The reader, another character, and the self.

a. A story that addresses the reader might address the reader explicitly.

> Believe me, dear reader, a story like this you haven't heard.

(These stories also tend to be explicit about the fact that a story is being told.)

Other stories that address the reader don't have to mention him explicitly at all. (Think of a standard story where the act of storytelling is never mentioned, like any of the examples I've provided you this semester.)

b. A story that addresses another character might go like this:

> I told you, Piney—don't shoot that bear. You did it, anyway. Now I'm rotting in this jail cell while you're running around the woods.

(Such stories often take the form of a letter or a letter-like monologue.)

c. A story that addresses the self will sound like a diary:

> How can I make it right with him? I didn't mean it! I didn't mean it!

And, in fact, these stories often take the form of a diary or a diary-like device. Note that the self is explicitly addressed, almost as a separate character, in this variant, while the reader is invited to observe the narrator's conversation with herself, like a bystander.

Let's review our questions and the possible answers:

1. Who's telling the story?
    a. first-person narrator ("I")
    b. third-person narrator ("he" or "she" or "they")
    c. second-person narrator ("you")
    d. collective narrator ("we")

2. How much do they know?
    a. omniscient (usually third-person)
    b. limited omniscient (third-person or first-person)
    c. objective

3. Part of the story?
    a. First-person: Yes
    b. Third-person: Yes or no

4. To whom is this person(s) telling it?
    a. reader (explicitly or not)
    b. another character
    c. self

I don't need you to memorize all these options. What I want is for you to understand the logic behind them. Doing so will help you develop an instinct for the best way to tell a story once you've come up with an idea for one, but briefly, there are lots of different ways to tell the same story.

Take my story about Trevor, the boy who won't get out of bed in Week 12 (show and tell). I can tell that story as an omniscient third-person narrator who could tell the reader what was really in Trevor's mind and what was in his mother's mind. I can tell it as a third-person narrator close to Trevor's perspective, in which case I probably won't be able to tell the reader what Mrs. Sanderson was thinking—I'm stuck in Trevor's mind. I can write it as an "I" narrator, from Trevor's—or Mrs. Sanderson's—perspective. I can write it in the form of a letter or e-mail to Mrs. Sanderson's husband who is out of town on business for several weeks, which will read very differently from a more conventional story employing dialogue, description, etc.

There isn't a single right choice that's immediately obvious to a seasoned writer. But developing an instinctive understanding of the options available is likely to take you a long part of the way. You may still have to try more than one approach, but you'll be skilled enough to understand sooner whether it's working or not.

This week's assignment is simply to go over the lesson one more time. This may be a disappointment to those who were planning on getting out of the assignment by finding a story featuring an "I" narrator who doesn't play some role in the story—but I'm here to tell you that none such exists, so you wouldn't have gotten out of it, anyway.

CHALLENGE EXERCISE

1. If you want to go further, produce an example of each of the 12 points of view classified above, each example ranging – like mine – from a sentence to a paragraph.

2. Look at your five favorite short stories or books and think about your five favorite movies. Write down, for at least three out of the 10, how each tells its story, using the classifications I introduced this week. Just answer, for each, the four questions:

   I. Who's telling the story?
   II. How much does the narrator know?
   III. To what extent is s/he a part of the story?
   IV. To whom is this person telling it?

If sometimes your answer is "I don't know," that's ok; not every story answers each.

GETTING AWAY FROM YOURSELF

Purpose: To practice writing from the perspective of characters unlike yourself.

This week, you will practice writing from the perspective of a character unlike yourself:

1. Someone of the opposite gender
2. Someone much older (or younger)
3. Someone whose viewpoint you disagree with

For your assignment, **you'll create a character profile for someone who's different from you** in one of the three ways presented above. Then **write a 500-word scene** using show, tell, or show-and-tell from that person's point of view.

How to begin? First, make sure you note that your assignment is *not* to simply write a character profile. You also have to write a 500-word scene in a story. You've been here before. Your first step should be to come up with a situation. Depending on which of the three out-of-body perspectives you choose, you'll need to come up with a scene that agrees with that person's experience. If you're writing from the perspective of someone 20 years older, a situation involving homework probably wouldn't make sense.

Fiction writers often set out to come up with a scene only to realize that a character profile has to come first because it will determine the story. (It is in this sense that some fiction teachers say, "Character is plot.")

So, let's back up and start by drawing three columns in our notebook: opposite gender, different age, and different beliefs. Now, fill each column (the whole notebook page) with observations about each type. Remember this lesson is on writing against type. Think as deeply as you can about what the life of someone of the opposite gender might be like. Observe a sibling of that gender, if you have one, or a friend; for someone of a different age, observe your parents as closely as you can for a day. Get out of your head and truly try to imagine yourself in the shoes of that person. What do their days look like? What are their tasks and responsibilities? What do they worry about? What are they responsible for? How do they relax? What do they enjoy? What are their dreams? If you're not sure, ask.

The same goes for the more challenging task of getting inside the head of someone you disagree with. Your disagreement can be about a place (you love hiking and camping, and this person hates it); it can be about belief (you're a liberal and your friend is a conservative, or vice versa); it can be about a book you hate and the other loves. The list is endless. Most of us don't have too many relationships with people who disagree with us on something of great importance. That's exactly why this exercise is so valuable.

A fiction writer's responsibility isn't to write about the things he likes, but to represent the world as it really is. A fiction writer is a seer, a truth-teller who looks deeper at life and draws attention to people, experiences, and ideas that, because of the close observation and meditation they require, most people don't usually notice. Part of that obligation is to render people as they are, not idealistically. Nothing exercises this skill better than having to get inside the head of someone you disagree with.

This doesn't mean that you have to find a way to agree with the person, but it does mean you have to find a way to humanize him and understand *why* he believes what he does. This skill makes us not only more capable fiction writers, but more empathetic human beings as well. We may not agree in the end, but there's no excuse for one-sided characterization. Few people are truly evil. Our job as writers and human beings is to understand how those with whom we disagree are people like us, who, more often than not, have thought long and hard about their beliefs and simply arrived at different conclusions. Fiction makes unthinking hate more difficult.

After you've drawn a character profile for your character, you're ready to tackle scene again. Perhaps drawing up the character profile suggested a situation, as that kind of brainstorming often does? For instance, my notes in the column about "person I disagree with or have negative feelings about" were about a friend with whom I had been planning a trip for a long time. I had done most of the planning because he was so busy at work, and I had laid out quite a bit of money for the trip. Also, many of the plans I had made for the trip were tailored to his work schedule. Then, at the last minute, he called to say he had to cancel because something had come up at work. I was very angry. I had spent so much time and money to plan this trip! My first impulse was to imagine that my friend wasn't being very thoughtful, ready to ditch a commitment.

But for the purpose of this exercise, I made myself imagine things from his point of view. I tried to imagine that he wasn't being cavalier about ditching our trip, in fact that he was genuinely regretful. I tried to imagine the kinds of things that could have come up at work to make him do such a thing. My friend works in politics and sometimes can't tell me everything about what he's doing, so maybe that was why he didn't explain very well why he couldn't go on our trip. And so on. Now, we don't have a situation for a story yet. But we do have a character profile from that person's point of view.

My next step is to come up with a scene that evokes this. The situation doesn't have to involve my relationship with this friend. It simply has to be told from this person's point of view. But it's legit to tell, show or show-through-telling this character's thoughts about having to forgo his trip with me as he gets ready for work one morning. Or I can purely show, by showing him involved with time-sensitive, secretive work, which implicitly demonstrates why it was ok for him to stay back. For instance, if I see him in a control room, helping the rescue of American soldiers from an ambush in Afghanistan, a top-secret situation that he couldn't tell me about, all of a sudden his inability to come on my trip doesn't seem so important, does it?

It's your turn. Go back to the top of the lesson and pick one of the types that's unlike you. (If you can come up with one that isn't on the list, feel free to use that one.) Your first step is to **come up with a character profile for this person. Then, place him or her in a scene using show, tell, or show-and-tell from that person's point of view.**

CHALLENGE EXERCISE

Do the same thing for the two other differences of perspective in this lesson.

CURIOSITIES AND FEARS: GETTING TO KNOW THE IDEAS WE HAVE ABOUT THINGS

Purpose: To understand how fiction helps explore the unknown.

How is it possible to get to know ideas that we already have?!

What I mean here is that we are filled with all sorts of preconceptions, fears, and curiosities that don't have a lot of justification. *How* we feel about something is far more at the forefront of our minds than *why*. You may dislike big social gatherings; be afraid of the dark; be curious about race-car driving; may worry you'll never fit in; may feel the pressure of being the first person in your family to go to an Ivy League college. That you feel those things may be a lot more obvious to you than *why* you feel them.

Things we're curious about tend to attract us; for instance, if you're fascinated by race-car driving, you probably spend a good deal of time on the Web researching drivers and their training habits. Conversely, you probably *don't* spend a lot of time thinking about or getting to know the things that turn you off or frighten you. After all, they turn you off or frighten you! Well, fiction can serve as an incredible tool to explore the unknown, be it positive or negative. It may pierce the bubble of an untested fantasy ("When I get to college, I am going to be the most popular guy on campus"), and it may take some of the sting out of a preconception or dislike. ("I don't like talkative people.")

As you have heard, fiction is all about detail. The more concrete a description is, the more vivid a picture it's going to conjure in the reader's mind. Fiction dies by generalities and abstractions like "I'm afraid of the dark." Afraid of the dark how? Give us a situation. Place a character in it. Take him through a story in which this fear factors significantly. Maybe he defeats his fear of the dark, maybe he doesn't. Perhaps the story isn't even directly about this. But I can guarantee you that your relationship to the subject in question will be different after you've written a story that touches on it. Writing it well will have forced you to get up close and specific with the subject in a way that generalized fear or anxiety prevents. It's like a dare that forces you to try something you've never tried before. There's even a cliché that applies: "Try it, you'll like it." Cliches are simplistic, and so you may find, after making yourself chat with a talkative person, that, actually, you're no fonder of talkative people than you were before. But that doesn't give you an excuse to represent a talkative person entirely without nuance and sympathy in a work of fiction. Fiction isn't exclusively a megaphone for the things you know and believe. It's also a way to explore the things you don't understand.

The same goes for positive subjects. A story that demonstrates the coolness and heroism of race-car drivers isn't going to be very interesting because it doesn't show the complexity that is part of every experience. Don't know the downsides about race-car driving? Spend some time learning about that side of the career. Maybe there's even a race-car driver you can interview, or something you read – danger of injury, long periods away from family, surprisingly low pay and glory for most of the competitors, the irrelevance of physical fitness – that will set your imagination off and give you new ideas you haven't read about. Getting this context doesn't and shouldn't destroy your race-car driving fantasy. But the exercise will have helped you develop a more realistic picture of what you're interested in.

To this end, this week, your assignment is:

1. Make a list, in two columns, of a) things you like and b) things that make you scared or anxious. Think about both for a while. Be honest. If you don't want to show your lists to your mentor, you don't have to.

2. Pick one to get closer to.

3. Do the research and brainstorming – online, in library books or magazines, through first-hand interviews, through imagination – that will help you learn more about it. If it's a positive curiosity, learn about its costs, downsides, risks, challenges, etc. If it's something that makes you unhappy, think about why. Think about people who don't respond to it in the same way. Try to understand why they don't. If you don't have a great deal of information about it, do some research.

4. Come up with a situation and characters that somehow explore the subject in question.

5. Write the opening of a short story (1000 words) that explores the situation.

We'll do a more formal lesson on effective openings next year, but for now, you should know that openings are a little bit different from the rest of the story. Openings often tend to be quite heavy on telling and background; they try to give the reader lots of information quickly so he can understand and appreciate what's going on. On the other hand, an opening could be just the opposite: disembodied dialogue between two people, with zero context about who they are, where they are, etc. It's the mystery of what's happening that keeps the reader reading.

If this assignment still feels abstract, let me give you an example of both a positive and negative unknown that I could explore in a short story.

As you may have gathered from my frequent references to the American West, I've had a great curiosity about it for a long time. I have lived in cities all my life, so maybe that's why. As a result, I developed all kinds of fantasies about the region—majestic landscapes, resourceful people, hard-working, taciturn, and even heroic characters. Where did I get these ideas? Probably from film Westerns. These ideas were so attractive that I never really doubted them. Oh, I'd heard that the myths about the West were just that—myths—and that it's a place filled with the same problems as any other place, but I didn't want to listen.

Then I made my first visit. During it, I saw some breathtaking things, and met some very unique people that fit no category I carried in my head. But I also nearly got trapped driving through a blizzard, which almost made me weep with terror; and in addition to those taciturn John Wayne types I'd thought about, I met some folks who weren't nearly as pleasant. It was also lonely, very lonely. I had failed to account for how accustomed I'd become to the noise and intensity of an urban environment. I left Colorado and Montana and New Mexico on those trips with a great deal of affection for the region, but I no longer believed that I could live there.

It won't surprise you to learn that I converted these experiences into fiction: A story about a man with some of the same interests as me who ends up in a blizzard, and because of the whiteout, runs over a man hobbling across a remote, rural road. (You might recognize this as one of your show-and-tell situations form Week 12.) He has to get him to a hospital to treat his bad injury, but it's hours away even in good weather. The rest of the story is about the two of them in that car. Here's how it opens:

The Saving of Curtis Purnell

Kaufman was so intent on the thunder coming out of the radio –

> "You work hard. *Reward* yourself!"
> "Those cravings *have to* come under control!"
> "End times for high prices!"

– that the first he knew of Curtis Purnell was when his Dodge hatchback took Curtis neat across the knees and deposited him several feet away on the slithering blacktop. Kaufman's chest knotted. The car continued to roll forward, the gentle motion harrowing in the wake of the impact. The car nearly rolled over the body before Kaufman snapped from his daze, freezing sweat already starting under his collar, and wildly rammed the gear-shift back and forth until it found P.

> The road was deserted, had been since Fort Garland. The passage from New Mexico into Colorado was like a turn of a switch, as if the level-straight lines separating the states on the maps Kaufman had studied so closely were for weather as well. The dun, bare peaks turned snow-streaked charcoal, and the sun was replaced by a bruised-looking sky that gleamed with mean silver light. All around him, the precipitation slowly but irreversibly made its way from rain to snow.

I was able to write a story exploring my newly complex feelings about the American West because I'd developed them on an actual trip there. You may not have the opportunity to test out a curiosity in the same way before you do this assignment. However, brainstorming can deliver some of the same results. For instance, make a point of interviewing some folks who hold different opinions.

Notice also that my story isn't directly about a love or fear of that open terrain. Kaufman, the urbanite, does come with all sorts of fantasies about the area, and his experience with Curtis certainly ends up disabusing him of some of them. But making the story directly about this would have been too on the nose. You need a situation—a **dramatic vehicle**, so to speak—that *shows* characters going through the same quandaries you're going through in your mind. At no point do Kaufman and Curtis talk about a "love of the West."

An exploration of a negative feeling would work along the same lines. One thing that gives me anxiety is the prospect of not being able to make enough money to live off my writing, and having to take on a profession that doesn't excite me nearly as much. I love working from home, making my own schedule, and doing what I love, so I imagine having to put on a tie and go into an office as a soul-sapping nightmare, and the people who do it as drones. This is unfair, to say the least. And it's high time I confronted the unfairness of this view.

Solution? Write a short story! But as we discussed above, it shouldn't explicitly discuss this issue; it should show it through characters in a situation. Maybe in my story a writer decides to write a story about an office drone. (It's a story inside a story!) Like any good writer, he decides to get some first-hand experience and gets himself hired as a temp at some firm. There, he discovers confirmation of some of the things he thought, but also unexpected positives. Maybe he falls in love; maybe he discovers himself to be amazingly proficient at some aspect of the company's business and helps it avoid a crisis. But he walks out of there a changed man in his views.

Note that this change oughtn't be "neat"—what he disliked before he loves now. When we have our mind changed about something, it usually changes in a way we didn't expect. My writer may still prefer to not work in an office, but his prejudices about it no longer look the way they did before the story started. Such a story might help me—and you, in this exercise—imagine a reality different from my unconsidered prejudice.

Your turn. Refer to the five-step guideline at the start of this lesson and write the opening to a short story that explores a positive or negative fear/curiosity.

CHALLENGE EXERCISE

Did you explore a curiosity? Do the same for a fear. Or vice versa.

FICTION • SECTION 6

STORY UNIT

WEEKS 17-18

REVISION

Purpose: To practice improving our fiction through a revision of already-produced writing.

It's the oldest excuse of any young writer: "I don't revise."

"Why not?" The teacher at the blackboard asks.

"It's more honest the way it comes out the first time."

For some reason, many young writers are under the impression that a story is like some kind of lightning: you capture it on the page, and then don't you dare touch it. You shouldn't succumb to this falsehood. Your writing, as I've tried to demonstrate over the past several years, requires forethought, patience, practice, and consideration. You can be sure that what you're reading now is far from the first draft of the syllabus. When *The Paris Review* asked Robert Lowell, the renowned poet, whether he revised, his answer was: "Endlessly."

That isn't to say that spontaneity, inspiration, and "being moved" play no role in fiction. They sure do. But those things are less predictable and calculable, and even when they arrive, you still need your craft toolbox to help make the most of them. (As someone I know likes to say, "The harder I work, the luckier I get.") Spontaneous, inspired ideas come to those who've been drafting, revising, and painstakingly sculpting.

Revised Draft

~~First Draft~~

In the concluding lessons of *The Creative Writer: Level Two*, I asked you to come up with the 5 Essentials for a short story: plot, characters, dialogue, setting, point of view. The following week, I asked you to alter one of those elements (and, in the challenge exercise that week, alter the rest). This was a way of getting you to revise, to imagine a different way for that part of the story to work.

Let's revisit the story opening I came up with in Week 12: I'll revise it in front of you. The revisions are in brackets.

> It was twenty minutes past the hour when Trevor usually got up [this phrasing feels a little bulky; what if I just said "past Trevor's usual hour"–that would still be clear, wouldn't it, considering what the rest of the sentence tells us?] that Mrs. Sanderson wondered why he wasn't at the breakfast table along with the other children. She had heard the alarm go off in his bedroom, she had heard it turned off. His oatmeal was on the kitchen table, getting cold. The other children chattered among themselves. [This is a repetition of "the other children" from above; by this point, the other children need names, or some other kind of identifying information. What about something like "Sarah and Bruce chattered among themselves, oblivious to their older brother's absence." And while we don't want to get too sidetracked – our job is to keep the plot moving along – we could stand to be more specific about what it is they're chattering about. What if they're chattering about Trevor's decision to stay in bed?! What if they already know about it because Trevor told them about it the previous night? As you can see, going over the first-draft details with a fine-toothed comb in this way – first-draft details that might have seemed perfectly fine initially – makes clear all the improvements/possibilities, large and small, that could be made/explored. So, what if that last sentence in this paragraph now reads: "Sarah and Bruce chattered among themselves, oblivious to their brother's absence, something about how could you go to the bathroom without leaving your bed." And that in turn, makes me think of another sentence to follow: "Bathroom talk having

no place at the breakfast table, Mrs. Sanderson made a note to change the topic as soon as she returned from stirring Trevor."]

Mrs. Sanderson put down her magazine and walked the carpet to Trevor's bedroom, feeling a lurch in her stomach. "Honey?" she said, knocking on the door and gently pushing it open.

Trevor was awake. He was brushing his teeth. In bed. Next to him, on a shelf where he usually kept the books he read before falling asleep, there were three cups: One [add: "empty, presumably"] for the toothbrush ["in his hand"], one filled with water, and one that he filled with the toothpaste water in his mouth. [This could be phrased more elegantly: "… and one he was using to spit out the rinse."] It was as if he had set them up the night before. ["Seeing his mother"] He placed his toothbrush in the first cup, took a gulp from the second, rinsed quickly, and dumped it in the third. [Just minor tweaks in this paragraph – clarifications, for the most part.]

"Hiya, mom," he said.

"Um, honey?" Mrs. Sanderson said. "What's going on?"

"I'm brushing my teeth," Trevor said. "What's it look like?"

"But there's a bathroom for that!" Mrs. Sanderson exclaimed. [The exclamation point makes perfectly clear that Mrs. Sanderson is exclaiming. No need to make that point over again. Switch to "said."] "Why aren't you at breakfast?"

"Because I'm here," Trevor said. "I'm not going to get out of bed today." [On reading this sentence a second time, it occurred to me that it might be more colloquial for Trevor to say "I'm not getting out of bed today."]

"Why not?!" Mrs. Sanderson exclaimed in horror. [It's good that I switched out the former "exclaimed" because this one would have been a repetition. But I don't like it for the same reason. Right now, three indicators – the question mark followed by the exclamation point, the word "exclaimed" and the words "in horror" are all doing the same "work" – making clear that

Mrs. Sanderson is scandalized. I can be much more concise: "Why not?!" and leave it there.]

Trevor gave this some thought, feeling the bristles of his toothbrush with his thumb. [On re-reading this sentence, it occurred to me that "gave this some thought" is superfluous. If the sentence read like this – "Trevor felt the bristles of his toothbrush with his thumb. 'I don't know,' he said finally." – wouldn't Trevor's action more or less convey the same information?]

"Trevor, you quit this right now. Up, up, up!" Mrs. Sanderson said and rushed her son's bed. [We can probably take out "said and" here. It goes without saying.]

What you've just seen is a crash course in revision: How revisiting a draft of fiction will make it better and better, because a first draft is concerned only with getting the details down. Later drafts can refine, the refinement going a long way. In this revision, no large-scale changes occurred to me: for instance, that the story would work better from another person's point of view, or that I should add a new character, or subtract one. But I did come up with quite a few minor changes that, taken together, will make this opening read much more effectively. If you want to test my hypothesis, present both versions to the mentor, and see which one s/he picks as the better. Your mentor may not even be able to say why, but I'm willing to bet s/he would prefer this version. In subtle but key ways, it's tighter, more vivid, more clever, less repetitive, etc.

Sometimes revision comes down to something fairly local like this, like word choice that could stand to be better. Sometimes, in rereading a story, you realize that something major has to change. You might decide that a character remains a little vague and needs to be fleshed out a bit more, either through show or tell. Or you might sense that a character seems altogether superfluous.

It's especially important to pay attention to impressions like the last. After having worked very hard on creating a character, you are going to be very reluctant to get rid of him or her. But if you're hearing that quiet voice say, "This character isn't adding anything to the story," try to listen. It may benefit the story. A really great but not very instinctive question to ask yourself as you revise is: "Can the story live without this detail/character/sentence/word"? If it can't, it can't. But asking will help you remove excess. It will also help you come up with better solutions. So many times, I've answered this question by saying: "This is necessary, but I just realized that it would be more effective elsewhere in the story."

We often avoid these difficult choices because we don't want to have wasted effort. But no effort is wasted. You'll be surprised by how this character reappears in another story of yours, already considerably fleshed out thanks to your previous work. Fiction practice never goes to waste.

A natural question might be: If I've just written it, and I consider it to be the best I can do, how am I supposed to revise it? Fair enough. Very often, as we're writing, we're subtly aware that certain things aren't as good as they can be, but we're so desperate just to get the basic facts down that we leave their improvement for later. But even if that's not the case and you aren't aware of what you can work on, you have other options:

1. Give the story or scene to your mentor for an objective look. Don't dismiss what he or she says. Writers don't have to take every suggestion from an editor, but only foolish writers ignore all. By virtue of working on the story for so long, and mucking around in the details so much, we've gotten so close that we can hardly be objective. Readers and editors like your mentor bring a fresh, more objective gaze.

2. See your story aside for a week; longer if you can handle it. When I was working on my novel I'd regularly set it aside for months at a time. This was invaluable in restoring some freshness to my eyes. When I came back to it, I would read it almost as if someone else had written it. That's the kind of experience that enables you to see what needs changing with less resistance on your part.

3. If you don't have a lot of time, simply rewrite the scene or the story from scratch. You can rewrite it with the same basic plot and structure, or you can purposefully try something different. But even if you choose to retrace your steps, I guarantee you're going to come up with something different. The act of thinking another time about the same questions is likely to yield more thoughtful answers. (Remember the Sensei Rule from previous levels: the second idea tends to be better than the first, and the third tends to be better than the second. This is also why the first draft is rarely the best.)

So, your assignment this week is to **revise the story opening you wrote for the curiosities-and-fears assignment last week.** Openings are tricky to revise because they don't necessarily look like the rest of the story. (And because it's often hard to revise until you know how your story ends. As an editor once told me, "You'll know what this novel is about once you've finished writing it.") So if you'd like, revise another scene from your practice this year.

CHALLENGE EXERCISE

1. Revise another piece of writing from this year.

2. Better yet, revise a piece of writing from previous levels. That should give you a lot more to work on.

3. For an even bigger challenge, pick several pages from a book you love and try to revise them.

WRITE A SHORT STORY

As always, we conclude our fiction section with **a short story in which everything is up to you. Last year, you wrote a story of 2000 words. This year, go for 3000.**

If you need help, why not expand the opening of the story that you wrote in Week 16 and revised in Week 17? Or you can work with any of the other openings or scenes you've produced this year. For a challenge exercise, start from scratch.

Remember the prep you can do:

1. Briefly revisit this year's lessons.

2. Flip through the basics from previous levels: how to conjure a character, how to come up with a situation.

3. Perhaps you might want to write a miniature version of your story in 100 words before tackling the 3000-word version.

4. Maybe you want to write a 1500-word one before trying to expand here and there.

Do try to incorporate as many of this year's lessons as possible. Try to write slightly more complicated stories and characters than what you've managed before:

- ☐ Stories where there isn't one clearly good protagonist and one clearly bad antagonist;
- ☐ Stories where the characters work against type to *some* degree;
- ☐ Stories full of detailed, concrete imagery, vivid language, and authenticating detail;

- Stories that show an awareness of whose perspective is guiding the story; and so on.

No challenge exercise this week beyond what's proposed in the lesson. Have fun!

POETRY

POETRY • SECTION 1

CRAFT PRACTICE USING A PUBLISHED POEM

WEEKS 1–7

HOW TO WRITE ABOUT [X]

Purpose: To figure out what "Feared Drowned" is about and how you might go about writing a poem like it.

In this first poetry lesson, we'll do what we did in Weeks 1–4 last year. We'll discuss what a poem is about, and how the poet might have decided to write about the subject in question—so that when you're sitting in front of a blank sheet of paper, you can get a little help from her example. With apologies to Sharon Olds—no one likes to have her poem manhandled by an outsider—we'll be using "Feared Drowned" as a lab experiment, rewriting parts of it to practice craft on our own.

Let's begin at the beginning. Let's read the poem.

Read the poem below out loud twice, slowly. Pause slightly, even if it seems strange to, at every comma (count to 1 in your head), period (count to 3), line break (count to 5), and end of stanza (count to 7).

Then have your mentor read the poem out loud, also twice, and following the same rules. Listen once with your eyes open and once with your eyes closed.

During your own first reading, focus simply on understanding what the poem is about. In the second reading, try to focus on the words and comparisons Olds uses in her descriptions. In the third reading (when your mentor is reading to you), think about the sound of the poem—are you hearing certain letters or sounds more than others? Does the poem sound "hard" (d, t, k, etc.) or "soft" (s, w, l, and vowels)? During the last reading, don't make an effort to focus on anything—just let your attention be drawn to whatever draws it. What caught your attention, either in the poem or outside of it?

Feared Drowned
by Sharon Olds

Suddenly nobody knows where you are,
your suit black as seaweed, your bearded
head slick as a seal's.

Somebody watches the kids. I walk down
the edge of the water, clutching the towel
like a widow's shawl around me.

None of the swimmers is just right.
Too short, too heavy, clean-shaven,
they rise out of the surf, the water
rushing down their shoulders.

Rocks stick out near the shore like heads.
Kelp snakes in like a shed black suit
and I cannot find you.

My stomach begins to contract as if to
vomit salt water
when up the sand toward me comes
a man who looks very much like you,
his beard matted like beach grass, his suit
dark as a wet shell against his body.

Coming closer, he turns out
to be you—or nearly.
Once you lose someone it is never exactly
the same person who comes back.[9]

Your assignment this week is to answer three questions:

1. What is this poem about?

9 Sharon Olds. "Feared Drowned." From *Satan Says*. Pittsburgh, PA: University of Pittsburgh Press, 1980.

2. How might Sharon Olds have come to write a poem like this?
3. If you were to write a similar poem, how would you go about it?

Don't worry about Questions 2 and 3 right now; let's just focus on 1—on understanding what this poem is about. I'd like your answer to be at least 250 words, written in a notebook. Afterward, you can look at my answer. Even if it seems like your answer needn't be as long as 250 words, do make it longer than a single sentence. Let your mind wander. Let yourself reflect on a broader set of issues than the narrow question I've posed. Think about the mood of the poem. Is it cheerful? Anxious? Full of anticipation? Confused? Think about the characters: who else appears, or doesn't, in the poem? For instance, does the couple have children? If so, why might they play such a small role in the poem? You should also think about whether you like the poem. (It's okay if you don't.) Think about why or why not.

One great tool of all writers trying to understand how or why something was written the way it was written is to think about what *isn't* in the poem, which is another way of thinking about all the other ways a poem could have been written about, say, a woman looking for a man on the beach. The poem didn't have to be written in this tone, in this mood, with this message. Imagining other ways for the poem to have been written helps us think about why it may have been written the way it was, and how your own approach might or might not differ.

So, your first question:

1. What is this poem about?

Compose an answer of at least 250 words in your notebook. Then, compare it with mine.

My answer:

At its most basic, this poem is about a woman's fear that her husband has drowned. Here, you have one answer to the question of what makes a good subject for poems: anything that provokes a strong emotion. You'll notice as well that Olds has chosen as her subject something akin to what I had you practice several weeks ago: an idea that makes us frightened or uncomfortable. Olds broadens that discussion. Here she tackles not an idea she disagrees with, or a concept that frightens her, but a personal fear: the fear of losing a loved one.

You'll notice how personal this poem is. It's not about the space program, or the price of tea in China. It's about a very private experience. In fact, Sharon Olds is known for writing about very personal subjects. Not all poets do. And some have even criticized her for it, saying it's self-absorbed. In my view, it isn't self-absorbed at all to write about personal experience; after all, it's what we know best. And chances are that other people have experienced similar things. Isn't the idea of losing a loved one frightening to you?

What else do we notice? Not only is the described experience private, it's also quite ordinary. I don't mean to imply that the risk of losing a loved one is no big deal. I just mean that, as I said about short stories, poems don't need extraordinary subjects: heists, life on other planets, deer with ten legs. The things right under your nose will do just fine. It's what you say about them that matters. Ultimately, the poem is about something much larger than that moment on the beach. It's about what it might be like to lose someone you love.

Here's how Sharon Olds herself has spoken about the way she writes (from an interview with the online magazine *Salon*): "I write the way I perceive, I guess. It's not really simple, I don't think, but it's about ordinary things—feeling about things, about people. I'm not an intellectual. I'm not an abstract thinker. And I'm interested in ordinary life."[10]

The subject of this poem could work as the subject of a short story as well—it certainly has more of a "plot" than most poems: a woman on the beach loses her husband; is he alive?—but a short story would look very different. For one thing, it would be hard to write a compelling standard-length short story with nothing more than an interior monologue from the woman. But it's just right for a poem. Poems don't have to be as story-oriented as short stories are. They get the reader interested by different means.

10 Interview published by Salon.com, July, 1996.

What are those means? Description, sound, and so forth—the craft skills that we'll be discussing in the weeks to come. But for now, let's move on to the second of our three questions.

2. How might Sharon Olds have come to write a poem like this?

There is no right answer here. We have no idea how she came up with the idea for the poem, and there's no revelation about it from me waiting for you at the end of the assignment. But it's useful to imagine because it helps you to understand how poems "come to us." It's a pretty elementary question, but a fundamental one, and if you're reading this guide, you probably want to ask it of yourself: What makes me want to write a poem? Is it being in a good mood? Is it having read or seen, whether in a magazine or in a television show, something truly wonderful and original that makes you want to try your hand at the same? Or, is it a powerful feeling about something, such as a sibling, the color of the sky at dusk, the story of the Civil War, or the unfair treatment endured by a slight boy in the neighborhood? (Notice that all of these prompts are **concrete**, or specific; we rarely get jazzed to write a poem about *justice*, or *greed*, or the color *yellow*, which are abstractions.)

So, in the same way, try to put yourself in the shoes of Sharon Olds and think about what might have inspired her to write this poem. Think of one scenario and write it down. Make your answer at least a sentence long, ideally closer to 5–7 sentences.

My own answer is below. Don't look at it until you write your own!

My answer:
I'd say Sharon Olds was on the beach with her husband or a friend one day, perhaps watching him emerge from the water. At that moment, she may have thought, What if he didn't come back out? How would that make me feel? That simple scenario, and the questions it may have inspired, might have led to this poem.

3. If you were to write a similar poem, how would you go about it?

This question takes off where Question 2 ends. Let's say *you* had the experience that you imagined Sharon Olds having prior to writing this poem. What kind of poem might you write about that experience? In answering that question, think about some of the issues discussed above: What would the mood of the poem be? What would happen in it (in other words, the plot)?

I know this may seem hard. Just as the sentence "Don't think of an elephant" makes you do precisely that, the instruction "don't write a poem like 'Feared Drowned'" makes you incapable of imagining another way to write about grief or losing a loved one in the surf of a beach. But try.

Imagining a different outcome for this poem is critical because it forces you to understand that there are lots of ways to write about the same thing. And it forces you to regard a published poem not as something written in stone like an ancient, sacred hieroglyphic that you have to decipher, but as a work in eternal progress that had to be stopped because the author was satisfied for the moment or it was time for publication.

(An aside: This brings us back to revision, which you've just finished in the fiction section. I've revised my novel eight times—that's 400 pages, rewritten over and over, down to the individual word level. Not incidentally, it's now 300 pages. I'll probably keep tinkering with it until a publisher takes it away from me, and even then I'll be kicking and screaming. But this also explains why so many poets about to publish a "Best of" rewrite the poems that go into it. Poems, like stories and novels, are eternal works in progress, and you should regard them as such. It's important to understand what a poem means, just as we tried to in Question 1, but as writers, we must also think about *how* the author came to write it as it is (Question 2), and how *we* would have written it if we'd gotten a crack at it (Question 3).)

So: Think about how you'd handle a poem—mood, plot, etc.—starting from the point where you imagined Sharon Olds starting in your answer to Question 2. Try to think of a style and plot for your poem that differs wildly from what Sharon Olds came up with but still makes sense. Could you write a poem called "Feared Drowned" that would be funny and get away with it? Jot down your brainstorming in a notebook. Go on for at least 150 words.

This practice will be of great use to you in Week 7. Trust me.

No challenge exercise this week.

A CLOSER LOOK AT DESCRIPTION IN "FEARED DROWNED"

Purpose: To use the poem to practice description.

If description in a poem were a fruit smoothie, it would have five ingredients:

- Imagery
- Concrete (vs. abstract) description
- Comparisons
- Close observation
- Specific vocabulary

In more detail:

Imagery: It may seem obvious, but a poem needs images. *Describe* things in your poem. Describe them in *detail.*

Concrete vs. abstract: Use the most specific words possible to describe something. Don't say "flower"; say "rhododendron."

Comparisons: A more detailed review follows later in this lesson, but for now, comparisons make something seem more vivid by comparing one thing to another. "My hand is a claw" is powerful because with a single word ("claw") it brings up associations of animals, or robots, or fear, or violence. Think of how differently you'd feel if the comparison was "my hand is a tree."

Close observation: Are you writing a poem about your Dad's pick-up truck? You'd better have studied its every dent and listened carefully to its every sound.

Specific vocabulary: Specific vocab is a bit like concrete language. If a particular bolt has a particular name, use that name – don't say "bolt." It will make your poem sound that much more authoritative, and make it that much easier for a reader to imagine herself in its world.

Having had this review, can you **give examples of how Sharon Olds uses the descriptive tools listed above in "Feared Drowned"?** This assignment will be Part 1 of this week's exercise.

For each of the five categories described above, make a column in your notebook. Try to provide at least three examples of each, if that many are available. (If not, don't worry too much.) Some of the answers may appear in multiple columns.

When you're finished, compare with my answer, below.

My answer (in narrative rather than column form):

Description/Imagery: "Bearded head," "too short," "too heavy," "clean-shaven," "water rushing down their shoulders," "rise out of the surf"—these are all detailed, specific descriptions.

Concrete vs. abstract: Note that Sharon Olds never uses the words "love" or "loss." You can't pour chocolate sauce on "love" or "loss." You can, however, pour it on a woman who can't find her husband. This poem takes care to use concrete language rather than abstractions. Rocks, kelp, salt water, sand, beach grass—these are all concrete.

Comparisons: This will be the subject of a separate exercise, but the poem is filled with beautiful, sharp, surprising comparisons: "your suit black as seaweed," "clutching the towel/like a widow's shawl around me," "his beard matted like beach grass."

Close observation: You can't have great description without close observation. I bet Sharon Olds spent quite a few minutes—if not hours or days, on and off—thinking about the rocks that stick out of the water before realizing that they could resemble the very head for which the woman in the poem might be looking. Isn't that a far more powerful comparison than if Olds wrote, simply, "Rocks stick out of the water near the shore" or compared the rocks to something out of context, like basketballs? Note also "suit black as seaweed," "suit dark as a wet shell," "kelp snakes in"—these are all descriptions that come from close visual observation.

Specific vocabulary: Just as in fiction, precision is critical. Kelp, seaweed, seal—they're specific words. They mean one thing only, and that's the thing that Sharon Olds wants to convey to her readers. Imagine if the poem said "your suit as black as that stuff that floats in the water" or "your bearded head slick as an *animal's*"—vaguer, isn't it? She says "beach grass," not just "grass." Her towel is a "shawl." These are all precise words.

Now for **Part 2** of our exercise.

We'll focus next on comparisons. Good comparisons are as critical to poetry as they are to fiction. In the first level of this series, I explained that the phrase "It snowed" is much less powerful than "it snowed so much that going to the mailbox felt like walking through water." The comparison helps the reader not only imagine the snow in his mind, but to feel it in his body, to imagine more vividly how much snow there was.

"Like walking through water," you may already know, is a simile. If you'd said, "I walked through an ocean of snow on my way to the mailbox," that would have been a metaphor. A simile compares two things using words such as "like" or "as." (For example, "He swung from the tree like a lightbulb.") Metaphors, on the other hand, compare two things by saying that one thing *is* another, not merely "like" it: "His belly is a basketball."

Metaphors don't have to take the form "X *is* Y." They can also simply use the language of one context in another:

- "crumpled carnation" (from the fiction unit)
- "The *mouth* of the oven disgorged the bubbling frittata."
- "The airplane *arrowed* through the sky."

Both similes and metaphors help us imagine what something is like by using the language of another image or feeling. But it's important to keep in mind what makes a good comparison. If you're writing about someone blue with cold, it would be silly to say "as blue with cold as a summer sky." A summer sky implies warmth, vitality, etc. Here, we're dealing with someone in the opposite state. We need a comparison to something that also evokes discomfort. So, "as blue with cold as fresh snow" (which sometimes has a bluish tinge), "as blue with cold as winter's dusk," etc.

For the second part of your exercise this week, **can you reread Sharon Olds' "Feared Drowned" and underline every comparison?** (Here's a hint: I counted eight. An underlined version follows this blank one, but don't peek.)

Feared Drowned
by Sharon Olds

Suddenly nobody knows where you are,
your suit black as seaweed, your bearded
head slick as a seal's.

Somebody watches the kids. I walk down
the edge of the water, clutching the towel
like a widow's shawl around me.

None of the swimmers is just right.
Too short, too heavy, clean-shaven,
they rise out of the surf, the water
rushing down their shoulders.

Rocks stick out near the shore like heads.
Kelp snakes in like a shed black suit

and I cannot find you.

My stomach begins to contract as if to
vomit salt water
when up the sand toward me comes
a man who looks very much like you,
his beard matted like beach grass, his suit
dark as a wet shell against his body.

Coming closer, he turns out
to be you—or nearly.
Once you lose someone it is never exactly
the same person who comes back.

Now compare your answers with the following:

Feared Drowned
by Sharon Olds

Suddenly nobody knows where you are,
your suit black as seaweed, your bearded
head slick as a seal's.

Somebody watches the kids. I walk down
the edge of the water, clutching the towel
like a widow's shawl around me.

None of the swimmers is just right.
Too short, too heavy, clean-shaven,
they rise out of the surf, the water
rushing down their shoulders.

Rocks stick out near the shore like heads.
Kelp snakes in like a shed black suit
and I cannot find you.

My stomach begins to contract as if to

vomit salt water
when up the sand toward me comes
a man who looks very much like you,
his beard matted like beach grass, his suit
dark as a wet shell against his body.

Coming closer, he turns out
to be you—or nearly.
Once you lose someone it is never exactly
the same person who comes back.

Were you surprised that I underlined "a man who looks very much like you"? Something that I found really interesting about this poem is the way in which *the subject of the poem influences the way the poem is written*: the author keeps **comparing** the swimmers she can see to the man she fears has drowned.

Part 3 of your exercise this week is to come up with new comparisons for Sharon Olds' poem. Here are the seven comparisons from "Feared Drowned" without their second halves:

1. your suit black as ____________
2. your bearded head slick as a ____________
3. clutching the towel like ____________
4. Rocks stick out near the shore like ____________
5. Kelp snakes in like ____________
6. his beard matted like ____________
7. his suit dark as ____________

Remember that you don't have to preserve the dark mood of Sharon Olds' poem. I'm not saying you should go for laughter, but feel free to play around. In thinking of comparisons, don't limit yourself. For instance, in the first one, your primary guideline is color: "Black as..." But you should also remember that you're comparing black swimming trunks, and the squareness of their shape can enrich the comparison. (Remember the discussion about dominant details from the first level.) That is, you could say "your suit black as night" or "your suit black as a box." A box doesn't have to be black, of course, but doesn't a pair of swimming trunks look like a square from a distance? I'm not saying this would make a good comparison; I'm just trying to get you to notice the different effects of these comparisons. Another option is to try to find a comparison that incorporates both the shape and the color, for instance "your suit black as a window at night" or just "your suit black as a window."

When you're done, rewrite the poem in your own hand using your comparisons instead of Sharon Olds'. How does the poem sound?

CHALLENGE EXERCISE

Comparisons are only one form of enriching description. Remember your other tools, reviewed earlier in this lesson:

- technical language
- concrete description
- vivid word choice
- close observation

See if you can come up with your own alternatives for at least one entry from each column you created earlier.

STANZAS

Purpose: To develop our understanding of stanzas through Sharon Olds' poem.

Let's start with a review of stanzas. Then we'll talk about stanzas in Sharon Olds' "Feared Drowned."

Poems are often divided into stanzas—that's the name for the six groups of lines you see in Sharon Olds' poem. "Stanza" is an old Italian word for "room, station, stopping-place." It's an apt word because the end of each stanza is meant to signal a breather in our reading of the poem.

Short stories and novels have breathers, too—ends of paragraphs, section breaks, ends of chapters. Same idea here. When we come to the end of a stanza, the poet wants us to take a deep breath. Where a poet chooses to start and end her stanza isn't casual at all. Neither is the number of lines she decides to include in the stanzas.

Where does Sharon Olds break up her poem into stanzas and why?

It's not an easy question to answer. Sometimes, it's very hard to say why a poet has chosen to end a stanza where she has. Sometimes a stanza doesn't "end," but, rather, cuts off in the middle of a sentence that the next stanza picks up. There aren't universal rules for what this means *every time*, but often, a poet will start a new stanza when something new happens in the action of the poem—a new scene, a new idea, perhaps a new sound. And cutting off a stanza midstride may be the poet's way of "leaving you hanging," making you rush on to the next one to see where the poem will go next.

It's counterintuitive, but we rush to the next line extra-fast if it's separated by a blank line—we work that much harder to keep in our minds what the last line said. Neat trick by the poet!

Also consider whether the stanzas have the same number of lines or not. A poem proceeding by a predictable number of lines in a stanza (be they four-liners or five-liners or what have you) creates a sense of order and rhythm. You *know* the next stanza will very likely have x lines. And if it doesn't, that's startling, an effective way of making you sit up and pay attention. It wouldn't have been as startling if every stanza had a different number of lines. If every stanza has a different number of lines, that breeds a sense of disorder, maybe even chaos.

Along the same lines of logic, very long stanzas feel heavy; stanzas of only one or two lines feel light. Alternatively, they might feel declarative because they concentrate in one or two lines the same amount of attention—a stanza's worth—that the reader will devote to a stanza with six lines.

Here is **Part 1 of your assignment. Can you come up with reasons why Sharon Olds may have divided her poem where she has?** Use your imagination and know that there are no right or wrong answers. Sharon Olds has her own reasons, but in some sense, they're none of our business. By taking up her poem, we acquire the right to come to our own conclusions. And that's one of the beautiful things about reading a poem—or appreciating any work of art, for that matter.

Review "Feared Drowned" with these questions in mind. Jot down your answers in your notebook. They can be as brief or lengthy as you like.

- ☐ Do Olds' stanzas have the same number of lines or not?
- ☐ What do you think that might mean?
- ☐ Do the stanza lengths create any particular kind of mood or feeling?
- ☐ Does it agree with the mood of what the poem is *about*?
- ☐ Do the stanzas end on complete thoughts or do they "leave you hanging"?
- ☐ Do the stanzas have many lines or few?
- ☐ What might each of these choices mean if you recall what the poem is *about*?

Finally, why do you think Olds ends her stanzas where she does? Try to come up with at least one possibility for each stanza in the poem.

I'll start you off by providing my answer to one of these questions. The rest are up to you.

My answers to the first set of questions...

The first stanza has 3 lines, as does the second. But the third stanza has 4 lines, the next stanza has 3, then 5, and finally, 4: 3, 3, 4, 3, 5, 4. It might look like there's no pattern to the number of lines in each stanza. The numbers seem all over the place.

But maybe that's *the point* here? This woman is discombobulated, mad with fear and grief. She isn't thinking clearly. The jumbled number of lines in the stanzas might be a small way for the author to indicate that.

Now, let's turn to **Part 2** of your assignment.

This week, we're going to practice creating stanzas by "rewriting" the lines in Sharon Olds' poem **in a new stanza combination.** That is, we're going to delete the stanza breaks in Sharon Olds' poem until we have a single solid block (of 23 lines). Then we're going break the poem into stanzas in a new way, though we'll have to think about why.

Start by rewriting Olds' poem in a notebook without any stanza breaks. If you have access to a computer, you can make your life easier by finding her poem online, copying it into a Word document, and playing with the stanza breaks there, without having to rewrite it every time.

Before you experiment with breaking the poem into different stanzas, consider the poem as consisting of a single stanza of 23 lines. How does this affect your experience of the poem? Stanzas are "stopping places"—we are meant to pause an extra-long beat between them. If this version has no stanza breaks, do we end up with a poem that reads more quickly or slowly? And, to place this in the context of what the poem is *about,* is the narrator experiencing something accelerated or leisurely? Also: Does the poem feel "heavier" or "lighter"?

As for breaking up the poem into stanzas (without changing any actual words or line lengths), think back to the reasons you came up with for Sharon Olds deciding to break her stanzas where she did. Think as well to the reasons why poets break up stanzas where they do, as discussed earlier in this lesson. Think about whether some of these reasons make more sense to you than the choices made by Sharon Olds. Maybe it's annoying to you that the stanzas don't have the same number of lines. Maybe it feels untrue to the poem's mood to have every stanza end on a neat little period, without breaking off mid-sentence and rushing along to the next stanza, the way a scared person's thoughts might. Or you could create new patterns out of the 23 lines, such as 11 two-line stanzas with a hanging last line. On one hand, this feels arbitrary—your choices should make sense considering the poem's content. On the other hand, if you're trying to understand why Sharon Olds' choices make sense, just rewrite the poem in a forced pattern, like the 11 couplets. It's invaluable for the same reason it was really helpful to imagine in Week 1 what Olds *hadn't* done in the poem. And you'll see how silly and forced the poem sounds. The poem is suddenly in the grip of a strange, archaic rhythm that has nothing to do with the events it details. The idea here is to see how differently a familiar poem reads depending on the organization of the stanzas.

Now for **Part 3**, the final element of the assignment.

After you've created your new version, **read it twice, and have it read to you twice by your mentor**, taking care to take a deep breath at the end of each stanza. In your notebook, **answer the bulleted questions I posed about Olds' poem** above about your own version.

After you're done, check out my try at the same challenge, below. If you find yourself needing some help, check out my answer first. Here's my stab at a rewrite, along with some notes about how I imagine the revised version's effect.

Feared Drowned
by Sharon Olds

Suddenly nobody knows where you are,

Your suit black as seaweed, your bearded
head slick as a seal's.

Somebody watches the kids.

I walk down
the edge of the water, clutching the towel
like a widow's shawl around me.

None of the swimmers is just right.

Too short, too heavy, clean-shaven,
they rise out of the surf, the water
rushing down their shoulders.

Rocks stick out near the shore like heads.
Kelp snakes in like a shed black suit

and I cannot find you.

My stomach begins to contract as if to
vomit salt water
when up the sand toward me comes

a man who looks very much like you,

his beard matted like beach grass, his suit
dark as a wet shell against his body.

Coming closer, he turns out
to be you—or nearly.

Once you lose someone it is never exactly
the same person who comes back.

I have a whopping 14 stanzas—more than double Sharon Olds'. Let's examine what I did:

- I liked the declarative announcement of the first line and decided to set it apart. Lines 2 and 3 were modifying that first line, so I made them their own stanza. (This made me want to end that first line on a period, if I could have my way with the punctuation.)

- The first line of the next stanza in Sharon Olds' poem—"Somebody watches the kids"—also has that full-stop declarative quality. So I decided to keep the pattern going. I isolated it, and then made the lines that refer to it ("I walk down…") their own stanza.

- Again, a declaration—"None of the swimmers is just right." And then again a modifying stanza: "Too short, too heavy…"

- What I found myself creating was a pattern of declarations followed by elaborations. About midway through the poem, however, this stopped working, so I preserved the pattern of one-line stanzas by other means. Every succeeding stanza seemed to me to have a line within it that deserved to be set apart. "And I cannot find you" is the hammer blow that succeeds the more even-keeled description that precedes it. "A man who looks very much like you" is a great revelation, a pause of a sort between the woman's nervousness ("My stomach contracts...") and the description of the man that follows ("his beard…). That pause is like the woman's held breath: Is it him? Is it him?

- I ended the poem on two two-line stanzas because they each seemed to hold a separate thought, and I thought the – again – hammer blow – of the last two lines needed its own breathing space.

How well did I do, do you think? I had fun, and I learned a good bit. I certainly thought a lot more closely about Sharon Olds' choices; but even though I think I made some interesting choices, the pattern I imposed on the poem seems at odds with the chaos of the woman's emotions. Also, it feels too full of the kinds of interruptions that you inevitably hear when you pause at the end of a stanza. Reading the poem felt like being in a bus stuck in traffic: An inch forward, then a sudden stop. The narrator is full of roiling thoughts rushing in worry: Such stop-and-go rhythm doesn't seem to fit the poem. If it wasn't clear from just looking at her poem why Olds' choice of stanzas was superior, this exercise suggests an answer.

CHALLENGE EXERCISES

1. Take a poem of your own and reorganize the stanzas. How do the versions compare?

2. Find a poem, either online or in a poetry book/anthology, whose stanzas do not end in complete sentences, the way they do in Sharon Olds' poem. Reorganize the stanzas so that they do. Does this new version read differently? How?

LINE BREAKS

Purpose: To understand the way line breaks influence the sound and feeling of a poem.

We've dealt with stanzas. This week, let's move on to the individual lines. How does Sharon Olds deal with line breaks? Where does she decide to end each of her 23 lines, and can we understand why?

Go back to the poem now and reread it.

The lines often don't consist of complete sentences; the sentences "run on" to the next line, so that you rush along with them, to figure out how they end. (Stanzas do this, too, you'll remember from last week, with the same effect.) This, too, mimics the author's emotional state, her thoughts rushing on: Where is he, where is he, where is he?

Note also the length of the lines. When your line doesn't end at the right margin of the page, as is the case with poetry, it can be very short—a burst of language interrupted by a lot of white space (silence) before the next line begins. But a line in a poem can be as long as one in fiction. Just look at the following poem, "Ponies," by a wonderful poet named C. K. Williams (an old professor of mine):

> When the ponies are let out at dusk, they pound across their pasture,
> pitching and bucking like the brutes their genes must dream they still are.
>
> With their shaggy, winter-coarse coats, they seem stubbier than ever,
> more diminutive, toy-like, but then they begin their aggression rituals,

ears flattened, stained brown teeth bared, hindquarters humped,
and they're savage again, cruel, all but carnivorous if they could be.

Their shoes have been pulled off for the season, their halters are rope,
so they move without sound, as though on tiptoe, though the rising mist.

They drift apart now, halfheartedly nosing the stiff, sapless remnants
of field hay -- sometimes one will lift and gaze back towards the barn.

A tiny stallion lies down,
rolling onto his back first,
then all the way flat.
A snort—rich, explosive; an
answering sigh: silence again,
shadows, dark.[11]

Doesn't the poem read almost like a short story? Sharon Olds' lines are brief, rushing along to the next line barely having completed the last. The ones here are long and flowing. Through shorter, anxious lines Olds makes us feel her narrator's anxiety. Again using the "what's not there" approach, think of how strange "Feared Drowned" would seem if it proceeded by the leisurely two-line stanzas by which "Ponies" moves along. That graceful, measured progress feels more right for "Ponies," which is itself about graceful, precisely maneuvering creatures.

Mary Oliver, a well-known poet and the author of *A Poetry Handbook*, points out that our lung capacity, as English speakers, is about 10 syllables. Anything longer than that requires a deeper breath and "suggests a greater-than-human-power. It can seem by its simple endurance… grandiose, prophetic. It can also indicate abundance, richness, a

11 C.K. Williams, *Collected Poems*. New York: Farrar, Straus and Giroux, 2006.

sense of joy."[12] Wouldn't those adjectives be apt for describing the timeless creatures in C.K. Williams' poem?

But in the end, these are just suppositions. Even if C.K. Williams were still my teacher, I wouldn't ask him why he used long lines in this poem. The wondering about the possibilities is the point, especially in poetry. It's a critical aspect of poetry that you must understand: Poetry concerns itself with the transmission of information even less than fiction does. It certainly wants to say something, but it doesn't always, or only, do it by telling a story. It does it much more by spurring sensations. Feeling out those sensations, playing around with them in your heart and mind, is sometimes more the point than figuring out what a poem is "about."

This week, we're going to do with line breaks what we did last week with stanzas: reorganize where the individual lines end, so that we can see what impact line breaks have on our experience of a poem.

Changing the line breaks in "Feared Drowned" requires us to talk a little bit more closely about where the lines break currently. Let's look at the first two stanzas again:

1 Suddenly nobody knows where you are,

2 your suit black as seaweed, your bearded

3 head slick as a seal's.

4 Somebody watches the kids. I walk down

5 the edge of the water, clutching the towel

6 like a widow's shawl around me.

I noticed that both lines 2 and 4 created a tiny bit of suspense at the end. "Your bearded" what? "Walk down" what? We rush on to the next line to find out, whereas at the end of line 6, the period brings us to a full stop and we take a breather.

There are so many ways you could rewrite the opening lines:

12 Mary Oliver, *A Poetry Handbook*. Boston, MA: Mariner Books, 1994, p. 41.

1 Suddenly nobody knows
2 where you are,
3 your
4 suit black as seaweed,
5 your
6 bearded head slick as a seal's.

1 Suddenly nobody knows
2 where you are,
3 your suit black as
4 seaweed,
5 your bearded head slick as a
6 seal's.

Can you point out what's different about these versions, judging by the criteria that we've been using so far—namely: Which moves faster? Slower? Do they have patterns? Do the patterns lend a certain rhythm to the poem? What information does each bump to the next line? Which has longer lines, which shorter? How well does each agree with the subject and mood of the poem? Perhaps most important, which do you like more and can you say why?

Your assignment this week is to rewrite the whole of "Feared Drowned" in two different ways. You don't have to change the line break in every single line, but try to change as many as you can. There's no right or wrong way to do this; there's no secret way to improve on the way that Sharon Olds did it. You are allowed to create patterns or just shuffle around words with no plan. I only want you to practice making this poem look different, as I did, and trying to see and feel how differently the poem sounds with different line breaks.

The rest of your assignment resembles your assignment from last week: **Read both versions aloud twice, followed by your mentor doing the same. Then fill one page in your notebook (about 250 words) with observations on how the poem struck you differently in each case.**

CHALLENGE EXERCISES

1. Take a published poem—if you're stuck, go online and find something by Mary Oliver, since we've been talking about her so much—and rewrite it so that every line ends with a finished sentence. Compare it to the original. How are they different? Judge by the criteria discussed in the lesson.

2. Take a poem you've written in full for a previous level of this series. Rewrite it, altering only the line breaks. Compare the effect of the two versions. Then show the two versions to your mentor, and ask him or her to do the same.

3. Create a new version of "Feared Drowned" which has no punctuation. How does it compare to the version that does?

4. Rewrite "Feared Drowned" as a piece of prose, that is, without line breaks – how you would see it if it was published in a short story. How does it read as a short story?

THE SOUND OF "FEARED DROWNED"

Purpose: To practice our understanding of sound effects in poetry using Sharon Olds' poem.

What do we talk about when we talk about sound in a poem? Re-read Goold Brown's lecture about the feelings inspired in us by certain sounds, which is included as Appendix A of this book.

Let's review what the earlier levels of this course covered about *sound* in a poem.

Soft vs. hard sounds

Sounds, just like words, have personalities. In an earlier level of this series, I asked you to come up with associations for words using the five senses. ("Determination" looks like…, sounds like…, tastes like…, etc.) Sounds have personalities, too. Vowels are "soft." Consonants are "hard." Certain consonants (l, s, w) are "softer" than others (d, k, t). If you're writing a poem about something leisurely and flowing, chances are it'll be heavier on the softer sounds. If it's about something frightening, or anxious, or tense, it might end up using a much "harder" set of sounds.

Sentence length

A frightening poem might also have shorter sentences that burst forth like barks, or screams, or criticisms, whereas a poem about something more majestic, like ponies, might have long, flowing sentences, with lots of curlicues, clauses, digressions, etc.

The poet Mary Oliver's *A Poetry Handbook* is a great resource for anyone who wants to understand this better. (For instance, see her dissection of Robert Frost's "Stopping by Woods on a Snowy Evening" on pp. 24-28.)

Repetition

Is there repetition in the Olds poem? Not so much, though I did want to mention the second line of the third stanza ("*too* short, *too* heavy..."). Don't those "too"s lend a drum-like rhythm to the poem: "too short, too heavy," dum-dum, dum-dum? And don't they recreate the chattering way we'll flip through and dismiss the wrong finds if we're trying to look for something or someone? Let's say your poem's about a boy who's lost the dog he's been asked to babysit and has come up with the bright idea of procuring a look-alike substitute at the pound. Standing at the window, anxiously looking for a twin, we might hear him say: "Too spotted, too gaunt, too furry, too jumpy..."

In the C.K. Williams poem in Week 4, the shape of the lines is identical, repeating from line to line. You might have a different feeling, but for me that creates a sensation of order and calmness, almost like a spell being woven over me and lulling me to sleep. This kind of repetition creates a rhythm, too.

Now for your assignment.

This week, you're going to explore "Feared Drowned" through the sound it makes. Your job will be to **answer the following questions in narrative or bullet-point form** in your notebook. **Each answer should be at least 100 words.**

1. What sounds does the poem make most frequently? Which are soft, which are hard? What kind of feelings do these sounds provoke in you?

2. Are Olds' sentences long or short? Why might she have made the decisions she has made?

3. Is there any repetition in the poem? Where? What feelings does it inspire in the reader?

My reflections on sound in the poem follow below. If you're struggling with your answers, have a look at them; otherwise, wait to read my work until you've finished your own.

Here, one more time, is the poem.

Feared Drowned
by Sharon Olds

Suddenly nobody knows where you are,
your suit black as seaweed, your bearded
head slick as a seal's.

Somebody watches the kids. I walk down
the edge of the water, clutching the towel
like a widow's shawl around me.

None of the swimmers is just right.
Too short, too heavy, clean-shaven,
they rise out of the surf, the water
rushing down their shoulders.

Rocks stick out near the shore like heads.
Kelp snakes in like a shed black suit

and I cannot find you.

My stomach begins to contract as if to
vomit salt water
when up the sand toward me comes
a man who looks very much like you,
his beard matted like beach grass, his suit
dark as a wet shell against his body.
Coming closer, he turns out
to be you—or nearly.
Once you lose someone it is never exactly
the same person who comes back.

I noticed a lot of *d*'s and *b*'s in the first words ("suddenly nobody"), followed by the softer *w*'s and the liquid semivowels of *r* ("knows where you are"). This makes sense. "Suddenly" and "nobody" are scary, harsh words. "Knows where you are" sounds more plaintive to me.

The next two lines are all about water, both literally—"your suit black as seaweed, your bearded/head slick as a seal's"—and aurally. They are full of liquid semivowels—*s* and *w*, over and over—though there is also the hardness of the *b* and *k* in "black," the *b* and *d* in "bearded." We have a real mix of the tender and harsh here, which makes sense: this is a woman afraid of having lost someone she loves, plus this is all occurring at the ocean, which can be soothing and destructive at once.

It's a *w* festival in the next stanza. Nonetheless, these lines feel harder than what we've experienced so far, as if the situation's getting scarier: The *b* and *d* in "somebody," the *tch* in "watches," the *k* in "walk," the *d* in "down." Every word is giving us something hard: e*dg*e, wa*t*er, *c*lu*tch*ing, *t*owel, arou*nd*.

Note that the world doesn't separate into "hard" and "soft," with appropriate sounds for each. You can write softly about an olive harvest (the appearance of the olives, the light, a family farm), or harshly (bruised fingers, long hours, etc.). A harsh-sounding poem about a bolt of lightning will convey its danger, speed, mercilessness. A soft-sounding one will focus the reader's attention on the snaking path of the light, the majesty of nature, the stunning illumination of the sky. Of course, a great deal depends on the content itself—on what you choose to say. But how you say it, the sounds you make, has a lot of impact on the reader, as well.

You should know that Sharon Olds didn't sit down with a preconceived plan to stuff her poem full of just the right balance of hard and soft sounds. Rather, through years and years of practice—listening closely to words, turning them over in her mind, paying attention to the subtle feelings they evoke—she developed a sharp instinct. **The words that come to mind for her as she's searching for good words to describe a woman looking for a potentially drowned husband are words that already pack an appropriate sound.**

CHALLENGE EXERCISES

1. Do what you did for "Feared Drowned" for a poem that you've written. Write 500 words.

2. From scratch, write a four-line poem filled with hard sounds about something soft. (For instance, a poem full of *d*'s and *k*'s about the water lapping a boat in the middle of the night.) Then write a poem that says the same thing, meaning-wise, but uses sounds.

THE SOUND/OF "DROWNED" (PART 2)

Purpose: To continue our sound practice by rewriting "Feared Drowned" as a rhymed poem.

Another way to affect a poem's sound is rhyme. Poems used to rhyme a lot more in the past, but practicing rhyme can be a great way to develop word skills, as well as an ear for how sound works in a poem. As Robert Frost once said, "Writing free verse"—unrhymed poetry—"is like playing tennis with the net down." That is, having to find words that rhyme makes us look harder and pay more attention.

It may seem unnatural to mangle this beautiful free-verse poem into a rhymed document. And rhyme, which lends a certain sense of order and regularity to a poem, may seem a strange choice for a poem about someone feeling such turbulent things. But you already know that forcing an unnatural choice on a poem—the "what's-not-there" trick—is a great way to understand just why the choice that the author did make is the *right* one.

Let's do a quick review of rhyme.

A **rhyme scheme** refers to which lines rhyme in a poem. The lines that rhyme with each other are denoted by the same letter of the alphabet. So, if the first and third lines of a first stanza in a poem rhyme with each other, they're both denoted by the letter "a." If the first and second rhyme with each other, then *they* are denoted by "a."

So, in the stanza

> In Week Six,
> we explore the sound
> of a little poem called
> "Feared Drowned."

The rhyme scheme is abcb. The first line is "a." The second line, which doesn't rhyme with it, is "b." The third line also doesn't rhyme with any, so it gets the letter "c." But the fourth rhymes with the second, so it also gets the letter "b." So would any other line in the poem that has a sound like "sound" or "drowned." What would be the rhyme scheme of this stanza?

> In Week Six,
> we break bones with stones and sticks.
> As we listen to the sound
> of a poem called "Feared Drowned."

If you said aabb, you'd be right.

Rhyme schemes are a useful way to get a handle on how poems can rhyme. For example, if every second line in a poem rhymes, that creates a much more orderly procession of sound than if every, say, sixth line rhymes. If every sixth line rhymes with each other, that still creates an echo of the rhyme in the poem, but very faintly. Just consider these two stanzas.

> In Week Six,
> we practice sound.
> We read a poem
> about a drowning
> And rewrite it full of rhymes.
>
> My house of bricks
> has a big, fat hound
> who's always home,
> lounging,
> full of burps and sighs.

The rhymes, though distant, create an echo of each other (six/bricks, sound/hound, etc.) but it's very faint—because the rhyme repetitions are separated by so many lines. Also, notice that some of my rhymes aren't perfect or exact, but **near-rhymes**; that is, they sort of make the same sound. (Drowning/lounging, rhymes/sighs.) Those are fine in poetry and have their own power.

On to this week's assignment. I'd like you to **rewrite "Feared Drowned" in rhymes.** The kind of rhyme scheme you use is up to you. You don't have to come up with one in advance; you could just write out the first two stanzas and play around, see what matches up with what. For instance, the starting two stanzas:

> Suddenly nobody knows where you are,
> your suit black as seaweed, your bearded
> head slick as a seal's.
>
> Somebody watches the kids. I walk down
> the edge of the water, clutching the towel
> like a widow's shawl around me.

could become:

> Suddenly nobody knows
> where you are,
> your suit black as **crows,**
> your bearded head slick as a **star**. [abab]
>
> Somebody watches the kids **while I call**
> **As** I walk down the edge of the sea,
> clutching the towel like a widow's shawl
> around me. [cdcd]

I made minor adjustments here and there to enable the lines to rhyme. The meaning of the poem has remained the same. (And should, as much as possible, in your version, too.)

Here's another option, preserving the length of the original opening stanza (three lines):

> Suddenly nobody knows where you are,
> your suit black as seaweed, your bearded
> head slick as a ~~seal's~~ **star**. [aba]

Here's another, using a near-rhyme:

> Suddenly nobody knows where you are,
> your suit black as seaweed, your bearded
> head slick as a tear. [aba]

[Note how "tear" tries to resemble both the shape and slickness of a wet head while serving as a near-rhyme for "are." Lots of balls in the air at once.]

Here are two final options:
(First lines of the opening two stanzas):

> Suddenly nobody knows where you are,
> your suit black as seaweed, your bearded
> head slick as a seal's.
>
> Somebody watches the kids. I walk ~~down~~ **far**
> along the edge of the water, clutching the towel
> like a widow's shawl around me.
>
> [abc ade]

Or (first and third lines of Stanzas 1 and 2):

> Suddenly nobody knows where you are,
> your suit black as seaweed, your bearded
> head slick as a seal's.
>
> Somebody watches the kids. I walk ~~down~~ **far**
> along the edge of the water, clutching the towel
> like a widow's shawl ~~around me~~ **as she kneels**. [abc adc]

These are not the world's most excellent rhymes, but they do give you an idea of all the different echoes a poem can create. I hope you read the above examples out loud.

There are 23 lines in the poem. Here's some guidance that should help focus the assignment:

- Do what you did in Week 3 and rewrite or cut and paste the poem into a single stanza of 23 lines. Don't worry about reproducing the stanza lengths exactly as in the original. Pretend you have a poem of one stanza of 23 lines, to be broken up by you as you see fit. (And, as per my first examples, you can increase or decrease the number of lines.) You have experience with this from Week 3. (If you want a challenge, you can try to rhyme the poem while preserving the original number of lines in the stanzas.)

- Aim for at least 10 lines to rhyme. Meaning that at least 10 of the lines should end in the same sound or near-sound as another line.

- You can have as few as two lines rhyming in a certain sound, or many more.

- Think about whether you want a pattern in your rhymes: Line 2 rhymes with Line 4, which rhymes with Line 6, and so on. Or Line 1 rhymes with Line 4, which rhymes with Line 7, and so on.

If you're struggling to do the assignment, then I'll assign you a rhyme scheme: Take the original 23 lines and convert them into a poem of six stanzas of four lines apiece. These stanzas should have the following rhyme scheme:

________________________________ (a)

________________________________ (b)

________________________________ (a)

________________________________ (b)

________________________________ (c)

________________________________ (d)

________________________________ (c)

________________________________ (d)

________________________________ (e)

________________________________ (f)

________________________________ (e)

________________________________ (f)

________________________________ (a)

________________________________ (b)

________________________________ (a)

________________________________ (b)

________________________________ (c)

________________________________ (d)

________________________________ (c)

________________________________ (d)

________________________________ (e)

________________________________ (f)

________________________________ (e)

________________________________ (f)

CHALLENGE EXERCISES

1. As you may have noticed by now, strict rhyme occurs very rarely in modern poetry. I believe that rhyme gets a bad rap these days, probably because when we think of rhymes we think of pretty stiff stuff, like John Donne's opening lines in "The Flea"

> Mark but this flea, and mark in this,
> How little that which thou deniest me is;
> It suck'd me first, and now sucks thee,
> And in this flea our two bloods mingled be.

Scattering rhymes more subtly through a poem—not every other line, but only once in a while; and not perfect rhymes every time, but near-rhymes; or using **internal rhymes**, which occur in the middle of a line rather than at the end—can suffuse a poem with a gentle, welcoming rhythm, like a light scent floating through the air, without overloading it with the hammer blows of precise, regular rhyming of the sort that crops up regularly in old poetry.

To that end, your first challenge exercise is to **do what you did to Sharon Olds' poem to one of your own** from this year or before.

2. Your second is to take an old rhymed poem like "The Flea" or one of Shakespeare's sonnets—if you'd like to work on something more modern and easy to comprehend, check out Robert Frost—and *remove* all of the rhymes; that is, find non-rhyming substitutes for all the words that rhyme while preserving the basic meaning. Apart from being a good way to develop your synonyms, this is another example of the "what's-not-there" trick—seeing how differently the poem would read and feel if it was composed in an entirely different way.

WRITE A POEM CALLED "FEARED DROWNED"

Purpose: To practice handling subject matter.

If you remember, one of your assignments in Week 1 was to imagine how you might write a poem with the same premise—a woman on a beach who suddenly can't find her husband. Well, **your mission this week is to write it.** Just make sure that you come up with something that differs from Sharon Olds' outcome in significant ways. What does "significant" mean?

1. Well, for starters, it should have a different "plot," for lack of a better word. Different things should *happen*. You can adjust the premise to: Person 1 can't find Person 2 on a beach. Who exactly those people are is up to you. And you can shift point of view as well. The narrator doesn't have to be Person 1. It could be a third-person, or off-stage, narrator, in which case the poem would refer to Person 1 as "he" or she," not "I."

2. Before you start, brainstorm about your poem in your notebook, using the criteria we've been looking at:

- **Description**: What images do you see when you think of the poem's premise? (They must be different from Olds' images.) Come up with concrete words for what you're seeing in your mind's eye. For instance, sand might be coating a sandwich you were eating until you realized you can't find whom you're looking for. Also, find a comparison that you might use in the poem. For instance, the sand under your feet might remind you of flour.

- ☐ **Lines and stanzas:** I often start my first draft of a poem by just writing stuff out and not worrying too much about the shape it has. Neither should you. But after you're done blurting out the poem, you might want to think about what your lines and stanzas are "whispering" to the reader—are they rushing on, or creating a feeling of slow, plodding progress?—and whether or not that works in tandem with what the poem is about.
- ☐ **Sound**: Keep in mind the general mood of your poem (funny? silly? tense? angry?) and think about whether the words you're using work against the mood (that is, the sounds are "soft" when the mood is fearful and tense) or for it.
- ☐ **Rhymes**: Do you want to include some in your poem?

No challenge exercise this week.

POETRY • SECTION 2

THE FUNDAMENTALS, WITHOUT TRAINING WHEELS

WEEKS 8–12

THE EIGHT WONDERS OF THE WORLD

Purpose: To write a poem featuring at least eight comparisons.

This week, you're going to work on a new poem, or re-work a poem you've already written, to include **eight** similes or metaphors, just like Sharon Olds' "Feared Drowned."

You've practiced comparisons quite a few times, and you've analyzed comparisons in a published poem, like "Feared Drowned." Now you're going to bring them into a poem of your own.

You should understand that a poem isn't required to have comparisons. There are powerful ways to describe that don't involve comparison. But skill with comparisons is a great tool to have.

I'd like you to do this lesson in **four** steps.

1. Come up with a subject for your poem. Remember to keep it focused, not abstract, and remember that it doesn't have to be grand.

2. Come up with a dozen words/ideas/entities associated with the subject. They could refer to place, thought, feeling, color, and much else.

3. Select a handful of these related aspects and try to come up with comparisons, using simile or metaphor. Create at least 10, so you can pick and choose for your eight. For a greater challenge, come up with only five, so that you have a good base, but leave some room for spontaneous discovery during the creation of the poem.

Understand that Sharon Olds probably didn't go down to the beach, draw up a list of the things she saw there–rocks, kelp, swimmers, seals–and then come up with several comparisons for each. You're going to do that this week because you're beginning your craft practice, as she did once. But its ultimate purpose is to hone your instincts so that comparisons begin occurring naturally to you. A hole-riddled t-shirt snapping in the wind on a clothesline becomes "a flag of surrender," mountains looming in the distance become "bowed heads," and so forth.

With these caveats, you're ready to begin writing the poem itself.

4. In composing the poem, remember that you don't have to begin at the beginning. Writing a poem is like unspooling a thread: you never know which spot on the ball of yarn the thread will poke out of. Your task is to grab it there and unwind. If you find yourself imagining with most ease a stanza that ends up being the last one, that's fine. If you're not thinking in terms of stanzas, but only lines, or even individual phrases, that's fine, too. To use a simile, think of the poem as a jigsaw puzzle. You almost never begin to put it together from a corner. You fill in a spot here, then a spot there, then maybe a linking image. And before you know it, a coherent image begins to peek through.

CHALLENGE EXERCISE

After doing this exercise, write the same poem—that is, on the same subject, and using as much of the same language as possible, and with the same power of description—*without any comparisons.* Remember the other description tools at your disposal.

SINGLE-LINE POEMS

Purpose: To understand and practice concision.

The idea for this exercise comes thanks to the poet Ted Kooser, whose book *The Poetry Home Repair Manual* talks about the poet's obligation to give readers a fresh view of the world. As an example, he mentions a one-line poem by Joseph Hutchison called "Artichoke":

O heart weighed down by so many wings.[13]

As Kooser justifiably says: Will you ever look at an artichoke the same way?

The Hutchison poem does more than just force a new perspective onto the viewer. It's an incredible example of many of the things we've been talking about: Concision, description via a fabulous metaphor, word choice, effective ending, and so forth.

However, I would agree with Kooser that its ultimate pleasure is the burst of discovery it provides: I would have never thought to describe an artichoke this way. (I probably wouldn't have paused to marvel at it closely enough to come up with such a description.

13 Used by permission of the author.

Hutchison did.) Would you agree that there's a great pleasure in being able to lavish such gorgeous description on something as everyday as a vegetable? That description ennobles the object of the poem, or maybe simply discovers the nobility that's been there all along.

This week, you're going to practice writing one-line poems. **Your goal is to come up with 10 one-line poems.** They don't have to consist of comparisons the way Joseph Hutchison's does. There are no requirements at all, except that you pay special attention to the way you end your line/poem, and generally take stock of the fact that you have only a single line to make your impact. So choose your words carefully.

How to prepare:

- Asked to write a story in six words, Ernest Hemingway famously—and perhaps apocryphally—replied: "For sale: Baby shoes, never worn." Rarely have six words said as much. Read authors known for publishing very short poems, such as William Carlos Williams. Or check out the book *Short and Sweet: 101 Very Brief Poems,* by Simon Armitage, featuring poems from 13 lines to none (!) at all. (The shorter ones are that much more striking, their single lines ringing 10 times as loud as the lines in a 10-line poem.)

- For an excellent, funny, and puzzling example, do an Internet search for "Siesta of a Hungarian Snake" by the Scottish poet Edwin Morgan. Poems like his, and Christopher Logue's "To a Friend in Search of Rural Seclusion" (also available on the Internet) lean toward **aphorism**, or clever sayings, expressed concisely. My favorite book of aphorisms is by another of my former teachers, James Richardson, Vectors: *Aphorisms and Ten-Second Essays.*

Remember the saying, presented in the fiction section, "This letter would have been shorter if I'd had more time"? Well, this week's exercise is the ultimate expression of that aphorism.

Now write those 10 one-line poems!

CHALLENGE EXERCISE

1. Write a two-line poem. Doesn't it feel really long by comparison?
2. Go in the other direction: Write a two-*word* poem.
3. Write a one-line poem that highlights sound, the way Edwin Morgan's "Siesta of a Hungarian Snake" does.
4. Write a one-line poem that highlights description, like Joseph Hutchison's ode to the artichoke.
5. In a preview of Week 11, write a one-line poem that has 10 syllables.
6. In a preview of Week 12, write a one-line poem which alternates accented and unaccented syllables. (A brief intro: In "bouquet," the first syllable (bou) is unaccented, the second (quet) accented. The reverse is the case in the word "**ran**-dom." Even three-syllable words can fit in this framework. Take a word like "de-**light**-ed." The middle syllable is accented, so that a line beginning, say, "**You**, de-**light**-ed…" has the desired order: accented, unaccented, accented, unaccented. More on this in three weeks. Dictionary.com can show you how to break up words into syllables.)

DEMOLITION DERBY

Purpose: To practice creating stanzas and lines by breaking up a piece of prose.

As we've discussed briefly, you could never mistake an old, rhyming poem for a piece of prose. The rhymes get in the way. They create their own rhythm and sound, utterly unlike a piece of fiction. With free verse—that is, poems that don't rhyme—that effect isn't as pronounced, and the author has to use different tools to distinguish it from prose.

Compare Robert Frost's "Mending Wall," reprinted below, with the poem that follows it, by Walt Whitman. Whitman was a pioneer of non-rhymed, colloquial diction in poetry at a time when rhyme was still king.

Read each poem out loud. Then, ask your mentor to read both poems to you out loud. Close your eyes while your mentor reads. Finally, take the book back and read my comments on the poems.

Mending Wall
by Robert Frost

Something there is that doesn't love a wall,
That sends the frozen-ground-swell under it,
And spills the upper boulders in the sun,
And makes gaps even two can pass abreast.
The work of hunters is another thing:
I have come after them and made repair
Where they have left not one stone on a stone,
But they would have the rabbit out of hiding,

To please the yelping dogs. The gaps I mean,
No one has seen them made or heard them made,
But at spring mending-time we find them there.
I let my neighbor know beyond the hill;
And on a day we meet to walk the line
And set the wall between us once again.
We keep the wall between us as we go.
To each the boulders that have fallen to each.
And some are loaves and some so nearly balls
We have to use a spell to make them balance:
"Stay where you are until our backs are turned!"
We wear our fingers rough with handling them.
Oh, just another kind of out-door game,
One on a side. It comes to little more:
There where it is we do not need the wall:
He is all pine and I am apple orchard.
My apple trees will never get across
And eat the cones under his pines, I tell him.
He only says, "Good fences make good neighbors".
Spring is the mischief in me, and I wonder
If I could put a notion in his head:
"Why do they make good neighbors? Isn't it
Where there are cows? But here there are no cows.
Before I built a wall I'd ask to know
What I was walling in or walling out,
And to whom I was like to give offence.
Something there is that doesn't love a wall,
That wants it down." I could say "Elves" to him,
But it's not elves exactly, and I'd rather
He said it for himself. I see him there
Bringing a stone grasped firmly by the top
In each hand, like an old-stone savage armed.
He moves in darkness as it seems to me,
Not of woods only and the shade of trees.
He will not go behind his father's saying,
And he likes having thought of it so well
He says again, "Good fences make good neighbors."

1861
by Walt Whitman

ARM'D year! year of the struggle!
No dainty rhymes or sentimental love verses for you,
terrible year!
Not you as some pale poetling, seated at a desk,
lisping cadenzas piano;
But as a strong man, erect, clothed in blue clothes,
advancing,
carrying a rifle on your shoulder,
With well-gristled body and sunburnt face and
hands–with a knife in the belt at your side,
As I heard you shouting loud–your sonorous voice
ringing across the continent;
Your masculine voice, O year, as rising amid the great
cities,
Amid the men of Manhattan I saw you, as one of the
workmen, the dwellers in Manhattan;
Or with large steps crossing the prairies out of Illinois
and Indiana,
Rapidly crossing the West with springy gait, and descending the
Alleghenies;
Or down from the great lakes, or in Pennsylvania, or on deck along the Ohio
river;
Or southward along the Tennessee or Cumberland rivers, or at Chattanooga
on the mountain top,
Saw I your gait and saw I your sinewy limbs, clothed in blue, bearing
weapons, robust year;
Heard your determin'd voice, launch'd forth again and again;
Year that suddenly sang by the mouths of the round-lipp'd cannon,
I repeat you, hurrying, crashing, sad, distracted year.

How would you compare the sound of the two poems? Neither rhymes, but they "tell their stories" in different ways, would you agree? To me—and you are entitled to see it a different way—Robert Frost's poem sounds a lot more like a piece of prose chopped up into lines of poetry. It has the diction of the kinds of sentences one might use in telling such a story to a friend. They're not perfectly vernacular—just look at the multiple clauses and description-heavy language of the first sentence, which takes up four lines. But the poem proceeds by complete sentences, formed more or less in traditional prose style.

This isn't to say that Frost wrote the poem as a piece of prose, then simply chopped it up into a poem. I'm sure he had his reasons for breaking the lines where he did. But you'll agree it reads a lot less "like a poem" than "1861."

"1861" is a trickier poem. Some, though not all, lines begin not flush with the left margin, but with an *indentation*. Some spill over into the next line while others don't. Note also that, after the exclamations of the first two lines, the poem has a single sentence. The poem is a tumbling rush of clauses, observations piling up on one another, descriptions (lines 3-8) interrupted by narrations of action (line 9 onwards) and so forth. The syntax isn't that of prose sentences; neither is the punctuation.

This week, you will try to make poetry out of prose. **In the first part of the assignment, you will chop up a piece of prose into two different "poems"** without doing anything other than breaking the lines. Imagine that you're a fashion designer and you have been given a big piece of fabric. Your job is to cut it up so that it looks like an elegant dress or a sharp suit. **In the second half of the exercise, you will pick the more promising of your two "prose poems" and rewrite it** to create some of the "only in poetry" effects that are so visible in "1861."

We'll use as our guinea pig an oldie-but-a-goodie from Level 2 of this series: "The Golden Goose" by the Brothers Grimm. Below are the opening lines:

> There was once a man who had three sons. The youngest of them was called Dullhead, and was sneered and jeered at and snubbed on every possible opportunity.
>
> One day it happened that the eldest son wished to go into the forest to cut wood, and before he started his mother gave him a fine rich cake and a bottle of wine, so that he might be sure not to suffer from hunger or thirst.

> When he reached the forest he met a little old grey man who wished him "Good-morning," and said: "Do give me a piece of that cake you have got in your pocket, and let me have a draught of your wine—I am so hungry and thirsty."

Here's your task:

Part 1:
Break up these lines into a poem of as many stanzas and lines as you'd like. Make sure you can justify to your mentor the reason for your choices. Then, repeat this process using different line breaks, such that you create a second poem.

When you're finished (not before!), you can look at my take on Part 1 of the assignment below.

My try: Version 1.

There was once a man who
had three sons.
The youngest of them was called
Dullhead,
and was sneered and jeered at and snubbed
on every possible opportunity.

One day it happened that
the eldest son wished to go into the forest to
cut wood,
and before he started
his mother gave him a fine rich cake and a bottle of wine, so that
he might be sure not to suffer from hunger or thirst.

When he reached the forest he met
a little old grey man who
wished him "Good-morning," and said:
"Do give me a piece of that cake you have got in your pocket, and let me
have a draught of your wine—
I am so hungry and thirsty."

My try: Version 2.

There was once a man who had three sons.
The youngest of them was called Dullhead,
and was sneered and jeered at and snubbed on every possible opportunity.

One day it happened that the eldest son wished to go into the forest to cut wood,
and before he started his mother gave him a fine rich cake and a bottle of wine,
so that he might be sure not to suffer from hunger or thirst.

When he reached the forest he met a little old grey man
who wished him "Good-morning," and said: "Do give me a piece of that cake
you have got in your pocket, and let me have a draught of your wine—I am so hungry and thirsty."

In my view, the first sample does the same thing every chance it has: Try to make you read on, faster and faster, by breaking the line right before some new piece of information is revealed. The first line ends right before we hear what we ought to know about this man who lived once. The third line breaks right before we learn what his youngest son was called. Of course, you're going to read on if this poem is an assignment or if you're naturally interested, but it's a small way of creating a tiny bit of suspense every time a new piece of information is about to be revealed.

The second sample stands out for having very long lines. (If you noticed, each stanza has five lines in the first sample and only three in the second.) What does reading *this* poem feel like? To me, it dragged. The original, as we've discussed, isn't particularly concise to begin with, and having to read it like a poem (slight pause at the end of each line) somehow only emphasized how long these lines are! It was almost like reading a short story, wasn't it?

Part 2:

Pick the version that you like more, the one that sounds the most "like poetry" to you, for one reason or another, and alter as much about it as you would like—punctuation, word choice, etc.—while leaving the meaning intact in order to create a more "poem-like" poem. The mentor will help you.

CHALLENGE EXERCISE

1. As is our pattern, in this exercise we use an existing piece of prose to convert into poetry. Write a "prose poem"—aka a paragraph of fiction—from scratch. (You can simply grab a paragraph from one of the stories you've written.) Then write the same poem much more "poetically": break up the lines, come up with stanzas, punch up the description and sound, etc. In other words, start out with something that looks like a piece of a short story and end up with something that looks a lot more like "1861."

2. Rewrite "1861" as a more prose-like poem: longer lines, full sentences, and so forth, along the criteria discussed up above in the comparison of "Mending Wall" and "1861." In other words, start with "1861" and end with something that looks a lot more like "Mending Wall."

LET US COUNT THE WAYS—ER, SYLLABLES.

Purpose: To practice meter, beginning with the most traditional: pentameter.

Think of this week's exercise as a marriage of the one-line poem exercise from several weeks ago (brevity) and the haiku exercise from last year's book (syllable-counting). We won't worry about **stress**—which syllables get *emphasized*—this week.

Let's back up for a moment: Why count syllables? You'll remember Mary Oliver's point that when speaking English, a single breath is good for 10 syllables. That doesn't mean that all lines have to be 10 syllables; it just means that consistently shorter lines will make us feel like we're spitting out the words, and very long lines (think of Walt Whitman) will make us feel like we're making a superhuman effort to say the whole thing in one breath. That our natural capacity is for 10 or so means that five will sound brief and 15 will sound lengthy.

This week, we'll get accustomed to seeing words as collections of syllables. Your assignment has two parts.

Part 1: Write out 20 random words from the dictionary and break them into syllables. Make sure you choose both short and long words. (A handy guide to rules for how to count syllables in English words appears at: howmanysyllables.com/howto-countsyllables.html.)

Check your work in the dictionary (or on dictionary.com). Dictionary.com also offers help with pronunciation. The dictionary often shows how to break up a given word into syllables, so keep your eyes off that if you can.

Part 2. Compose 10 lines of poetry—each line independent and having nothing to do with any of the others—each of which has 10 syllables. (Your individual words can be as long or short as you want them to be.) You can use any or none of the words from the first exercise in this lesson.

Hint: Begin by not worrying about the syllable count. Just get the basics of a line down. Then work with synonyms, syntax, etc. to arrive at the number of syllables you need.

That's it. Go to work.

CHALLENGE EXERCISES

1. Variation on the exercise: Write 10 lines that make sense together. That is, write a 10-line poem where each line has 10 syllables.

2. Practice for next week by underlining the accented syllables in your 10 distinct lines of poetry (and in your 10-line poem, if you did challenge exercise #1.)

3. Break up the following 20 words into syllables. If you don't know the definitions of any, please look them up.

- [ ] pulchritude
- [ ] shenanigans
- [ ] versatile
- [ ] elegant
- [ ] boombox
- [ ] journalistic
- [ ] everlasting
- [ ] meritorious
- [ ] despicable
- [ ] mandalay
- [ ] bake
- [ ] brutal
- [ ] aerie
- [ ] rhythm
- [ ] moonroof

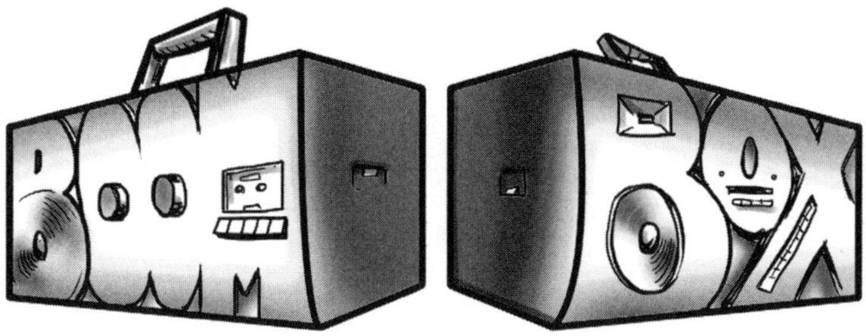

- [ ] delinquency
- [ ] susurrous
- [ ] separation
- [ ] fury
- [ ] amoeba

THAT'S A LOVELY ACCENT YOU HAVE!

Purpose: To begin to learn about stress in poetry.

Let's start here: Read aloud this line, from Shakespeare:

> If music be the food of love, play on.

Write it on a separate piece of paper, then ask your mentor to read it out loud to you. As you listen, circle every syllable that, to your ear, seems like it gets emphasized during pronunciation. This is a subtle skill, so don't be frustrated if you don't make out any differences. However, you know that in the word "mu-sic," it's the first syllable that gets emphasized, and here's a handy tip for the rest of the line: "Meaty" words like food and love are often going to get more attention during pronunciation than connectors, like "the" and "of."

First, let's count the syllables:

1	2	3	4	5	6	7	8	9	10
"If	mu	sic	be	the	food	of	love,	play	on."

So, this is an example of **pentameter**: ten syllables. Let's break that down.

In this line, there are ten syllables. But the syllables belong together in pairs. Each pair of syllables is known as a **foot**. So "If mu-" is the first foot of the line, and the other four feet are...

sic be
the food
of love
play on

the entire line has *five feet.* That's called **pentameter.** (If each line had only two feet, the meter would be called **dimeter.**)

Let's continue by bolding those syllables that seem to get emphasized during reading:

"If **mu**-sic **be** the **food** of **love**, play **on**."

Think figuring out the emphasized syllables is hard? Make it easier for yourself by purposefully accenting the "wrong" syllables:

"**If** mu-**sic** be **the** food **of** love, **play** on."

Doesn't it sound horrendously awkward? As a writer friend of mine once advised me, one of the best ways to conquer your fear of getting a bad result in writing is, ironically, to try to achieve it. This is the "what's-not-there" trick we've been discussing. If you're not sure what the right answer is, try another answer. It might be so wrong that it'll reassure you that you had the right one originally.

The technical name for emphasis on a particular syllable is **stress.** An emphasized word is **stressed.**

Dividing a line by its syllables and the **stresses** each syllable receives is called **scansion**. Our scansion of the Shakespeare line above suggests that it has alternating stress. The line starts with an unaccented syllable, then has an accented one, then repeats the pattern four more times, like this:

da-DUM da-DUM da-DUM da-DUM da-DUM

if MU sic IS the FOOD of LOVE play ON.

Compare this line to another that means more or less the same thing:

"**Mu**-sic is the in-spi-**ra**-tion for **ro**-mance."

Which of the two lines feels more rhythmic or sing-songy? Can you smack the table in unison to either one? The first one, for sure: da-DUM, da-DUM, da-DUM, da-DUM, da-DUM. It has 10 syllables—as we've discussed, the measure of an English speaker's breath—and it alternates da-DUMs perfectly.

da-DUM pairs of syllables—an unaccented syllable followed by an accented one—are called **iambs** (AH-yams). Iambs are the most powerful accent pairs because they mimic the beat of our hearts: da-DUM, da-DUM, da-DUM, da-DUM, da-DUM.

So this line is *iambic pentameter* because there are five sets of syllables ("feet") and each set of syllables has an unstressed-STRESSED (da-DUM) pattern.

Other syllable combinations:

There are other syllable combinations:

- "**Ran**-dom" is a **trochee**: A heavy stress followed by a light.
- A **dactyl** is a three-syllable unit, in which the first syllable is stressed, and the next two are not. Example: Syllables 1–3 and 4–6 in "**Now** is the **win**-ter of **our dis**-con-**tent**" (Shakespeare, *Richard III*) make up dactyls. The title of William Faulkner's novel "**Ab**-sa-lom, **Ab**-sa-lom!" is a pair of dactyls as well.
- An **anapest** is the reverse: Two light stresses followed by a heavy one, for instance "'Twas the **night**..."
- In a **spondee**, as you saw above, both syllables receive the same stress. "Our dis" in "our discontent" is a **spondee**.

You don't have to memorize these terms now. But do note that accenting in poetry is a little different from accenting in speech. In grammar, the word "discontent" gets only one stress: "dis-con-**tent**." But in poetry, more than one syllable in a single word may be stressed, such as here. It all depends on how the line is read and what the author wishes to emphasize. (What the author wishes to emphasize, however, will always contend with our natural tendency to read in iambs.)

No single right answer all the time:

It's possible to read the same line in different ways, and meter specialists often disagree on the proper way to scan a line. For instance, the online Shakespeare Resource Center scans "**Now** is the **win**-ter **of** our **dis**-con-**tent**" this way. (And Shakespeare's "A **horse**! A **horse**! My **king**-dom **for** a **horse**!", also from *Richard III*, can be rendered "A **horse**! A **horse**! My **king**-dom for a **horse**!") All the same, there are some constants. You'll agree that in "Now is the winter of our discontent," it makes a lot more sense to emphasize, in the opening syllables, "now" rather than "is" or "the."

Stress in pronunciation depends greatly on what we mean. The same sentence can be rendered in a half-dozen different ways, as a helpful example from Wikipedia shows:

> *I* didn't take the test yesterday. (Somebody else did.)
>
> I *didn't* take the test yesterday. (I did not take it.)
> I didn't *take* the test yesterday. (I did something else with it.)
> I didn't take *the* test yesterday. (I took a different one.)
> I didn't take the *test* yesterday. (I took something else.)
> I didn't take the test *yesterday.* (I took it some other day.)

For a more poetic example, check out the opening lines of Robert Frost's "Birches":

> When **I** see **bir**ches
> **bend** to **left** and **right**
> A**cross** the **lines** of
> **straight**er **dar**ker
> **trees**,
> I **like** to **think** some
> **boy's** been **swing**ing
> **them**.

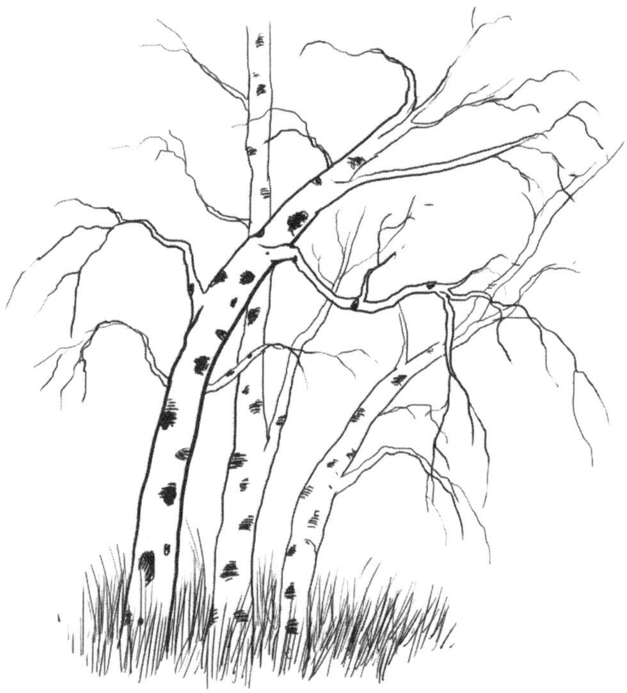

Notice that "I" gets the accent in line 1 (these lines are written in iambic pentameter) but not in 3, because that line's emphasis is not on who's doing the seeing—that's been established—but, rather, on the emotional state of the viewer.

Think of stress as a living organism, shifting shape with every example depending on what the speaker means. That makes it a more challenging concept, but one with richer potential as well. Deploying stress creatively can lead to poetry with rhythm that, like a great song, echoes in your ears long after you've put the poem down.

A word of guidance:
Figuring out stress is one of the most complex tasks in poetry, so don't be frustrated if you don't quite get it from this lesson. It's a skill developed over many years, and even advanced poets often don't possess it in full. The best thing to do this week is to hunker down and just do all the exercises assigned, main and challenge, without worrying about whether you're "getting" it. It's only through repetition that patterns start to emerge. By the time you're done with this week's assignments, I bet you'll have a far better instinct for meter than when you started. (Believe it or not, it may even have become fun in the process.)

This week's assignment:
This week, we're going to stay focused on iambs. Note that pentameter is not the only way to write in iambs. An iamb makes a single **foot**. A line of poetry consisting of **one** iambic foot is said to be in iambic **mono**meter. By the same logic,

- A line of poetry consisting of **two** iambic feet is said to be in iambic **di**meter.
- A line of poetry consisting of **three** iambic feet is said to be in iambic **tri**meter.
- A line of poetry consisting of **four** iambic feet is said to be in iambic **tetra**meter.
- A line of poetry consisting of **five** iambic feet is said to be in iambic – you got it – **penta**meter.

This week, your assignment will be to **practice creating iambs**.

1. Start by coming up with five two-syllable iambs—five lines of iambic monometer.

2. Then create four four-syllable lines (dimeter) —four lines of iambic dimeter.

3. Then three lines of iambic trimeter. (Can you guess what that means?)

4. Then two lines of iambic tetrameter.

5. Finally, a single line of iambic pentameter, like our two examples from *Richard III.*

It may help you to have some training wheels. Look over poems and fragments of poems you've written this year, and use them as your departure points. It shouldn't be too hard to come up with five lines of iambic monometer, as there you're basically looking for two-syllable words, or two one-syllable words where the emphasis clearly falls on one rather than the other. Here are five examples:

1. For-**give**
2. Re-**turn**
3. Grace **us**

Note that this line can go either way depending on the context:

a. **Grace** us **with** your **pre**-sence, **Lord** Al-**migh**-ty (pentameter consisting of trochees, not iambs)

b. Grace **us**, not **them**, the **wic**-ked **beasts** (iambic tetrameter)

4. Bring **forth** (almost every time, the emphasis is going to be on "forth")
5. Se-**date**

Your four-syllable iambs can consist of anywhere from one to four words:

mag-**nif**-i-**cent**
Lieu-**ten**-ant **Smith**; The **dis**-con-**tent**
The **ba**-sic **rule**
And **then** they **wept**

Make sure that you read your lines out loud. That's the only way to make sure that you've chosen words with the correct stresses.

CHALLENGE EXERCISES

1. Scan the following Shakespeare sonnet. That is, break it up into accented and unaccented syllables. Hint: it consists largely of iambs. Your extra challenge is to figure out which four spots depart from iambic meter. (For an analysis of the poem's meaning, check out: shakespeare-online.com/sonnets/145detail.html.)

   SONNET 145
   Those lips that Love's own hand did make
   Breathed forth the sound that said "I hate"
   To me that languish'd for her sake;
   But when she saw my woeful state,
   Straight in her heart did mercy come,
   Chiding that tongue that ever sweet
   Was used in giving gentle doom,
   And taught it thus anew to greet:
   "I hate" she alter'd with an end,
   That follow'd it as gentle day
   Doth follow night, who like a fiend
   From heaven to hell is flown away;
   "I hate" from hate away she threw,
   And saved my life, saying "not you."

2. Write a poem of 10 lines in iambic pentameter.

3. Write a poem in which the first stanza is in iambic monometer, the second in iambic dimeter, the third in iambic trimeter, and the last one in iambic tetrameter.

4. Scan Sharon Olds' "Feared Drowned," a more complicated exercise than scanning the regular meter of a Shakespeare sonnet.

POETRY • SECTION 3

BACK TO NONSENSE

WEEKS 13–17

BRAND-NAMERS FOR A DAY

Purpose: To explore sound through the names given to commercial products.

Things have been pretty serious for the last couple of weeks. It's felt like an English class in here! It's time to loosen up and get back to another important rule of poetry: Beware of rules. The next five weeks, we are going to revisit, and advance, the "nonsense" practice from the last volume in this series.

As we've discussed, a poet draws as much inspiration from—and pays equal attention to—the sound of words as their meaning. In the next several weeks, we are going to live in a universe without meaning(s). You will explore

- the effects of sound in the absence of meaning and
- the beautifully non-rational meanings created by the insertion of foreign and invented words.

This week, you're going to moonlight as an advertising executive. Your job is going to be to name, or rename, ten well-known products. Then, you're going to invent new names.

This may seem like a strange exercise in a creative-writing textbook, but if you think about it, most products on our shelves don't have names that mean something. Their names are pure sound—sound meant to evoke certain feelings in the consumer. Even when their names do mean something, such as BlackBerry, their connection to the named product is anything but literal. So, unexpectedly, advertising—or, more specifically, branding—is a great way to study sound and the feelings certain sounds and words evoke without being distracted by meaning. This will be our focus for the next five weeks.

To give you an example from my life, I used to work at a start-up company related to travel. I was asked to try to come up with a name for it. I thought and thought until the idea struck me: Oyster.com. Why "oyster"? Oysters have nothing to do with travel. And yet: Oysters suggest luxury. There is also the expression "The world is your oyster," which is certainly related to travel. "Oyster" rolls off the tongue. And it can easily become a verb, just as "Google" did, as in "Did you Oyster that?" meaning "Did you look that up on the Oyster site?" My bosses liked the name and the company is named Oyster.com to this day. Check it out online.

One other great way to prepare for this week's exercise is to read the article "Famous Names" by John Colapinto in the October 3, 2011 issue of *The New Yorker* magazine, accessible online at newyorker.com.

The final step of your preparation for this week's exercise to peek back at Goold Brown's lecture on sound from last year's poetry section, included as Appendix A in this book. The values and feelings he assigns to particular letters are exactly what you'll be thinking about this week.

This week, you will **a) come up with 10 existing products that you will rename, and b) come up with new names for products that I will provide.**

Here's a list of "existing products." These aren't the product names I'm going to provide for the b) part of this exercise--just an example for you.

Examples of existing products:

1. Kleenex (tissues)
2. Tide (laundry detergent)

3. Maytag (washing machine)
4. Panasonic (electronics maker)
5. Chick-fil-A (restaurant chain)
6. Tropicana (orange juice)
7. Energizer (batteries)
8. Patagonia (outdoor wear)
9. Jansport (bookbags)
10. Saturn (cars)

You can see the appeal of some of these names. Tide brings up water, and water is cleansing. Panasonic feels futuristic because of the -sonic. Tropicana brings up warmth and sun because of the tropica-. Energizer works the same way. Patagonia is an area of rugged beauty in Chile. Jansport is sporty. Saturn is light and futuristic. In all these cases—except Maytag, perhaps—the meaning of the word or part of the word is the key element. But that doesn't have to be the case. The solar-energy company Solyndra ran into some trouble with the government recently, but it still has a memorable name. Solyndra makes me think of the sun ("sol" means sun in Spanish, but it's so ubiquitous that it's almost an English word by now), so nature, and by extension, solar energy, which is the company's business, after all; cylinders, which feel technological (I imagine men and women in lab coats and hard hats); and spaceships, so a general sense of the future (perhaps because of that "a" at the end, which feels like a spaceship firing off into the beyond). Voila—great name.

Now you need to come up with 10 names of your own.

Part 1:

Once you've selected 10 product names to work with, **choose a *new* name** for each of the products. Try to find a name that evokes the same associations for that product. For instance, Dirtex isn't the way to go with a replacement for Kleenex!

In coming up with new names, start by jotting down associations for the product. For instance, for a washing machine, I'd write down words like: clean, tumble, dry, clothesline, fresh air, sun, water. You could get less literal and write down the feelings evoked by clean laundry: "new start," or perhaps "childhood" (because our moms used to do our laundry then, and yours probably still does, lucky you.)

- You can rename the product using a word from your associations: Tumbler.
- You can combine two words: SunTumbler, FreshStart.
- You can combine fragments of various words: Sunline. ("Line" is vaguely electrical and invokes machines like washing machines). As a contrast, SunTumb might not be so good because "Tumb" sounds like "tomb."
- Or collect the sounds common to some of the words above—c, -l, -m, -s— and make a whole new word from them: Celamis.

Part 2:

For Part 2, **please name the following items:**

1. Breakfast cereal consisting of dried cherries, prunes, and bran
2. Vitamins that strengthen the immune system
3. Running shoes
4. Spaceship
5. A new town in Florida
6. The first town on the moon
7. A shipbuilding company
8. A ship
9. A toothpaste that tastes like candy (but is good for you!)
10. A baseball team from your hometown

If, reading, say, #8, you think "But what kind of ship? You'd name a speedboat something very different from an aircraft carrier," you'd be very right, indeed. Whenever an option feels too general – abstract! – come up with a more specific variant.

CHALLENGE EXERCISE

Spend this week paying close attention to every brand name you encounter. Keep a log in a notebook. Spend at least 50 words making notes in your notebook about the feelings evoked by the name, investigating the component words (if any) as well as the individual letters and sounds.

AN APPLE A DAY… OR A FOREIGN WORD PER LINE

Purpose: To see how the insertion of foreign words affects the sound of a poem.

It's time to loosen up and get back to another important rule of poetry: Beware of rules. The next four weeks, we are going to revisit—and advance—our "nonsense" practice from last year. Poetry, as Ted Kooser reminds us in *The Poetry Home Repair Manual,* is about seeing things anew. You can't do that if you don't let go of convention now and again.

The sound of words can feel inseparable from their meaning. Take the word "crafty" – it sounds to me like someone stealing around a corner. "Drafty," even though it shares every letter but one, sounds like a wind coming from under a door. But what about a word like "parabens," or "alto-forno"? I don't know as readily how I feel about those (Portuguese) words. This set of exercises asks you to think about it. More accurately, to *feel* about it.

The inspiration for this week's exercise comes from Kenneth Koch, whose book *Sleeping on the Wing* I referred to in Level Two of this series. We will build on this exercise in the weeks to come. What's the exercise? Replace one word per line in a written poem—either by you or a published one that you like—with a word in a foreign language. Do you know any foreign languages? Don't use words from that language! Since the point here is to separate sound from meaning, use words from a language you *don't* know.

Here's the assignment: Find a poem, either one you've written this year or a published on you love (extra credit if you write one from scratch!) and **replace one word per line with a foreign word.** Then translate the words back into English and rewrite the poem for an absurd variable on the original. This exercise has a two-pronged objective: 1) To explore the *sound* effects of foreign language, and, in terms of meaning, 2) to discover the wonderfully absurd poems that foreign words can lead us to.

How to do this?

Imagine that the first two lines of your poem are like the following (made-up) lines:

> What a sad moment,
> the first winter day when the sun doesn't appear.

Then pick a language you don't know. Find online a source of words from that language, such as a news outlet, and choose a couple of words to use in your poem. Then insert away, wherever you feel like in the line, one word per line. My search brought me, in Portuguese, "parabens" and "alto-forno."

> "What a *parabens* moment,
> the first day of *alto-forno* that the sun doesn't appear."

Doesn't the introduction of these foreign words create a new sound and feel for the lines?

After you're done, look up the meanings of your foreign words, and rewrite the poem in English for a very surprising and fresh-sounding result:

> What a *congratulations* moment,
> the first day of the *blast furnace* that the sun doesn't appear.

The lines don't make rational sense, but they provide delight nonetheless: the delight of surprise. "Congratulations" is the last word we expect to see before "moment." So this pair of lines has caught our attention and left a mark despite its lack of traditional logic. It has a cryptic beauty all the same. It is this kind of delight and fresh perspective for which poetry aims. Even better if the selected word doesn't agree syntactically with the rest of the sentence (e.g. "the first day of the *pretty* that the sun doesn't appear").

When your poem is finished, read it out loud to your mentor. See how those foreign words affect someone else!

No challenge exercise this week.

DEFINE *THIS*!

Purpose: To experiment with sound by inventing English words and using them in a poem.

Last week we filled our poems with words from foreign languages whose meanings we didn't know. This week, you're going to fill your poems with words you're going to *invent.* It's another way to free our minds from their focus on meaning (and prepare you for next week's more challenging version of this exercise).

How to invent a word?! Perhaps you've had words you wished were "real" kicking around your mind. In my case, I've always wished that "anticipation" had an adjective, so you could say "I'm very anticipatious" or "anticipatory" instead of saying "I'm looking forward." Same goes for "trepidatious." Why *doesn't* "trepidation" have an adjective form?

For this assignment, we need words that are *wholly* invented. Words like:

mouzhy

croop

stoozer

clid

speesh

gunny

hod

What do they mean? I'm not sure. I just like their sound. This week, you'll come up with some of your own. It's fine to use inspiration from existing words. I came up with "hod" because I mistyped "hood" in an e-mail.

Part 1:

The first part of your exercise is to **invent at least 10 words**. Then, you will take a poem you've already written or a published poem we've looked at previously, such as "The Owl" by Alfred, Lord Tennyson, and **cross out one word per line**, just like last week. (Which word is up to you – you can cross out randomly, or not.) Then, **sub your invented words for the words that have been removed**. (If your poem is, say, 16 lines, you will need to come up with 16 words, not 10.)

Have the poem read to you, your eyes closed. What's it like to have a poem with meaning transformed into a document where sound is more primary?

Variation: Invent your words *after* crossing out the originals, trying to invent words that "sound" as if they would mean the same thing.

Part 2:

Of course, poetry is usually a marriage of sound and meaning, not purely random sound. In this next part of the assignment, you will start by **coming up with definitions** for your 10 (or however many) words, as if you were the original author of a new language, deciding what words should mean.

How to define a word? Inevitably, your definition may be colored by "real" words the word sounds like. An invented word like "graditate" will remind you of "grade," "gradual," "graduate." All of those are ok, but feel free to range further afield. Maybe you get stuck on the fact that the "g" looks like a girl in a swingset. (Maybe in your language the meanings come from the *appearance* of the first letters. You're free to sustain that kind of pattern, though it runs you into trouble when you encounter other words beginning with "g.")

You can also be completely random or comically specific in your definitions. There's no reason "graditate" can't mean "to rain sideways" or "to twist your foot on the first step you take in a given day."

In English, words often gain their meaning from their roots (in Latin, Greek, or other languages) or perhaps historical moments that brought the word into our lexicon. In your language, the word meanings can have any logic you like.

Part 3:

The final step of this part of the exercise is: Write a poem using your invented words and the definitions you've come up with, making as much sense as possible.

CHALLENGE EXERCISE

As the assignment is quite lengthy, no challenge exercise this week.

WRITE A POEM IN AN INVENTED LANGUAGE

Purpose: To take our practice of sound-without-meaning still further.

Last week, you invented enough words to sub a word per line in a poem written in English. This week, your objective is to go even further: to write a *whole* poem in an invented language.

Here's perhaps the most famous example of poetry in an invented language, Lewis Carroll's "Jabberwocky." The opening and closing four lines are pure invention.

(from *Through the Looking-Glass, and What Alice Found There*, 1871)

`Twas brillig, and the slithy toves
Did gyre and gimble in the wabe:
All mimsy were the borogoves,
And the mome raths outgrabe.

"Beware the Jabberwock, my son!
The jaws that bite, the claws that catch!
Beware the Jubjub bird, and shun
The frumious Bandersnatch!"

He took his vorpal sword in hand:
Long time the manxome foe he sought --
So rested he by the Tumtum tree,
And stood awhile in thought.

And, as in uffish thought he stood,
The Jabberwock, with eyes of flame,
Came whiffling through the tulgey wood,
And burbled as it came!

One, two! One, two! And through and through
The vorpal blade went snicker-snack!
He left it dead, and with its head
He went galumphing back.

"And has thou slain the Jabberwock?
Come to my arms, my beamish boy!
O frabjous day! Callooh! Callay!'
He chortled in his joy.

`Twas brillig, and the slithy toves
Did gyre and gimble in the wabe;
All mimsy were the borogoves,
And the mome raths outgrabe.

As Alice says after reading the poem,

> "It seems very pretty,... but it's rather hard to understand!... Somehow it seems to fill my head with ideas – only I don't exactly know what they are!"[14]

You can say that again.

Note that Carroll doesn't invent crazy words like "aldukraa" or what have you. His "gimble" and "uffish" are only a shade removed from real words like "nimble" and "oafish." (Though "manxome" is pretty out there, isn't it?) They may not mean the same thing, but he gives himself a leg up in this way.

Later in the book, Carroll has the character Humpty Dumpty explain the invented words to Alice. His explanation gives you a glimpse into what Carroll was thinking when he created those words:

> "'*Brillig'* means four o'clock in the afternoon -- the time when you begin *broiling* things for dinner."
>
> "That'll do very well," said Alice: "and *'slithy'*?"
>
> "Well, *'slithy'* means" `lithe and slimy.' `Lithe' is the same as 'active.' You see it's like a portmanteau -- there are two meanings packed up into one word."
>
> "I see it now," Alice remarked thoughtfully: "and what are *toves*?"
>
> "Well, *'toves'* are something like badgers -- they're something like lizards -- and they're something like corkscrews."
>
> "They must be very curious creatures."
>
> "They are that," said Humpty Dumpty: "also they make their nests under sun-dials -- also they live on cheese."
>
> "And what's to *'gyre'* and to *'gimble'*?"
>
> "To *'gyre'* is to go round and round like a gyroscope. To *'gimble'* is to make holes like a gimlet."

14 Thanks to the site jabberwocky.com, run by David Shaw, for drawing my attention to Alice's response.

"And *'the wabe'* is the grass plot round a sundial, I suppose?" said Alice, surprised at her own ingenuity.

"Of course it is. It's called *'wabe,'* you know because it goes a long way before it, and a long way behind it—"

"And a long way beyond it on each side," Alice added.

"Exactly so. Well, the *'mimsy'* is 'flimsy and miserable' (there's another portmanteau for you). And a *'borogove'* is a thin shabby-looking bird with its feathers sticking out all round -- something like a live mop."

"And then *'mome raths'* ?" said Alice. "If I'm not giving you too much trouble."

"Well, a *'rath'* is a sort of green pig: but *'mome'* I'm not certain about. I think it's short for 'from home' -- meaning that they'd lost their way, you know."

"And what does *'outgrabe'* mean?"

"Well, *'outgribing'* is something between bellowing and whistling, with a kind of sneeze in the middle: however, you'll hear it done, maybe -- down in the wood yonder -- and when you've once heard it you'll be *quite* content. Who's been repeating all that hard stuff to you?"

Your job this week will be to **write a whole poem in an invented language.** You can do this in a whole bunch of different ways:

- You can turn on a recorder, close your eyes and ears, and make funny sounds. Then transcribe them, figure out where to break the lines and stanzas, and voila – you have a poem.

- You can invent a bunch of words, as you did last week, and then make each the anchor of its own line of poetry. (Exactly how is up to you.) Then, cohere these individual lines into a poem of multiple stanzas.

- Just write from scratch—the #1 approach, but without bothering with a tape recorder.

- Take a poem you've written or a published poem we've studied and change every word in some consequential way. So, the opening lines of "The Owl"

When cats run home and light is come,
And dew is cold upon the ground,

for me, became:

Whoo ceists ra hame und lij sae comesy,
Und doy sae cloets upayne dai grent,

For some reason—perhaps because I've just started reading a novel with Dutch characters, or because English shares so much with Dutch—I found myself giving a Dutch tinge to some of my invented words ("cloets").

I also found myself establishing something of a language! I already had words for "and" and "is"—"und" and "sae"—when I encountered them in the second line. That was fun.

You'll notice I kept the general length of the words, so the new poem is as rapid and staccato as the original. You didn't have to do that. Your first line could have read:

Whifta ceistekine ra hamelekin und lij sae comesistai,

But then, note how the sound of the line changes. Even when we're not dealing with "real" words, the issues of syllable, rhythm, and accent remain. In fact, it's a purer challenge as we're not being diverted by meaning. Even though I don't know what the line above means, I can tell it's a bad one: too many syllables. The tongue trips over them.

You may choose to rhyme your lines, if you wish. Pay attention to syllable, accent, and rhythm. But most of all, pay attention to the sounds made by the poem—that's all you've got with a language you don't know. "Aldukraa" is awkward (though perhaps not to a speaker of Afrikaans or Finnish, both of which have many repetitions of the same vowel next to each other). The name "Adriana" is less awkward, the "a"'s at the end have musical echo. Same goes for a name like "Adelaide." The "d's" speak to each other. (Rare names like "Adriana" and "Adelaide" are a good way to practice sound. They're not made up words, but they're not predetermined by semantic associations, if you don't know anyone by those names.)

The length of the poem—the number of stanzas, the number of lines—is up to you. Aim for at least 16.

CHALLENGE EXERCISE

Let's have a fiction refresher. Write a dialogue between two characters in an invented language.

TRANSLATE A POEM FROM A FOREIGN LANGUAGE

Purpose: To increase our awareness of sounds.

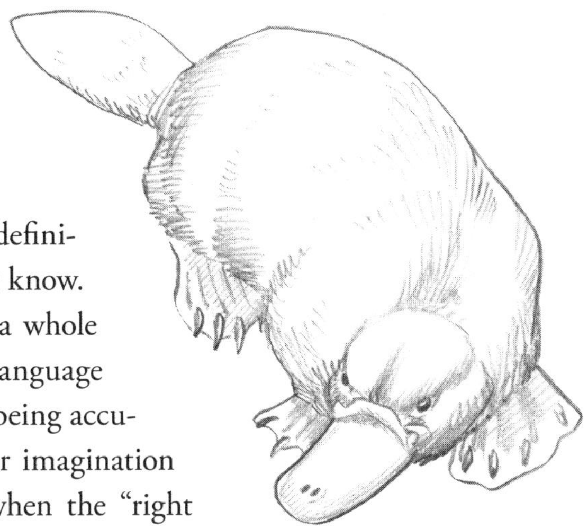

This exercise also asks you to come up with a definition for something whose meaning you don't know. Except that now, you'll have to do that for a whole poem. How to translate something from a language you don't know? First off, don't worry about being accurate. That isn't the point here; it's to let your imagination roam, to get it accustomed to wandering when the "right answer" doesn't matter.

Read the original several times and take careful notes every time something comes to mind while reading. For instance, maybe you picked a Spanish poem. If the Spanish word *platicar* makes you think of a platypus, that's great. Jot it down. It doesn't matter that it means something else. If the line, "Es tan corto el amor, y es tan largo el olvido" makes you think of *tans*, the word *large*, or *olive oil*, or you happen to know that "amor" means "love," so be it. Anything goes.

Having read the poem several times and made notes about what it brought to mind, use a page of your notebook to brainstorm about a way of connecting the dissimilar things of which the poem has made you think. Don't think of the poem as either making sense or not making sense; making sense only some of the time is fine. But do try to impose as much order on the poem as you can. That order doesn't have to do anything with meaning such as "the poem is about a hunt for mushrooms deep in the forest on a day of approaching bad weather." You've done plenty of exercises listening to sound rather than meaning; your order can be **aural** (having to do with sound) rather than **semantic** (having to do with meaning). The first letter of every line can be the same, or the last letter; or the letter "b" can be missing from the entire poem and it's a poem about a thirst for honey. (Get it?) If you find yourself wondering, "Would it be ok to...", just know the answer is yes.

If you happen to recognize or guess some words in the text—you can probably guess that "fuerza" means "force" in Spanish and "magnifique" means something like "magnificent" in French—all the better. Now, you actually have a shot at decoding the poem as a whole. It's an entirely distinct and interesting challenge to try to string together random decoded words ("force," "necklace," "magnificent," "revenge") into a (semi-)sensible poem. In some ways, this leaves you with less freedom than you'd have if you recognized or guessed none of the words.

Here is a brief excerpt of a poem in German (by Rainer Maria Rilke, a great German poet), a language I don't know, my translation of it, and an explanation of how I arrived at the choices I did.

> Mit allen Augen sieht die Kreatur
> das Offene. Nur unsre Augen sind
> wie umgekehrt und ganz um sie gestellt
> als Fallen, rings um ihren freien Ausgang.
> Was draussen *ist*, wir wissens aus des Tiers
> Antlitz allein; denn schon das frühe Kind
> wenden wir um und zwingens, dass es rückwärts

> All the creatures in existence
> Offend you. Our unsure existence
> Is one of grief, and confusion, and loss of sense.
> We fall down the rings until we tumble through the exit.

What *is* this world of tiers of ever-greater struggle?
We feel like aliens, apart from our own kind,
We stride in solitude, each in his own quiet forest.

How in the world did I come up with this sad little ditty?! Well, it was hard to ignore that Kreatur probably meant "creatures" or "Creation." I couldn't resist the association of Offene to "offend" even though I knew the two probably had nothing to do with each other. And by then, the main idea of the translation was set: In short, why is life so hard? I couldn't even guess what "umgekehrt" and "ganz" and "gestellt" meant, but I already had a theme going, so I made up definitions within its context: "grief," "confusion," "loss of sense." Why not?!

Let's see what the accurate translation of the poem is (by Brian Cole):

Every creature sees with all its eyes
wide space. Our eyes alone are as if
reversed and placed around like traps,
placed at every exit they might find.
What there *is* outside we only know from the face
of the animal, because we turn round and force
even the very young child to make him see

Ok, I didn't get very close except for a general atmosphere of unease, but that's ok because that wasn't the point of this exercise.

Use a foreign-language poem of your own choosing. You have several options in translating the poem:

1. Read the poem several times. Read it to yourself, read it aloud, have it read aloud to you. Jot down some notes about the feelings the poem evokes. Don't be swayed by preconceptions about languages and cultures. German words sound sharp-edged compared to the soft sh's and zh's of Portuguese, but Germans write poems about love and Portuguese write poems about long dark nights of the soul, too.

If you've managed to arrive at a set of feelings inspired by something about the poem —the tone, the sound—you can use those feelings to inspire your translation.

2. You might go through the poem word by word, trying to come up with *related* definitions for each (offend, dark, etc. in my Rilke segment above), or at least enough as I did—to power a translation. Maybe you'll recognize a word because it's similar in English.

3. To create a translation in the absurd tradition, pick 10 words out of the poem and come up with *unrelated* definitions for them. Write a poem that strings them together.

Now make your own translation.

CHALLENGE EXERCISE

For a wonderfully absurd poem in English, write a poem in a foreign language you don't know. Find a series of words in an online dictionary of that language or the website of a newspaper in that language—don't peek at definitions if they're available—and then just string those words together based on nothing more than sound. Then, once you have a full poem, translate it into English.

POETRY • SECTION 4

FREE POEM UNIT

WEEK 18

WRITE A POEM

Purpose: To write a poem incorporating any, or as many, of this year's lessons as possible.

As has become our custom, the last assignment of the year is a poem whose subject and craft specifics are up to you. Do try to write a poem that demonstrates as much of an understanding of this year's lessons as possible. Use descriptive tools such as similes and metaphors, and describe closely. Think about where you end your lines and why. Think about the organization of your stanzas. Think about the rhythm of the words you choose, their syllables and accents, and how the words and lines sound next to each other. I don't mean you should diagram your poem. I mean that you should try to keep these lessons in mind as you start to work on the poem. It's one of those situations where you should refresh your recollection of this year's lessons, then set your notes aside, and write from scratch. I hope that enough of the guidance will have seeped in that it travels from your conscious awareness to your instincts. If it hasn't, that's fine. Honing this passage is a lifelong process for most creative people.

CHALLENGE EXERCISE

None.

MENTOR'S NOTES

Start by getting the writer to attribute words to already-known qualities of the character in question. Ask: How would you describe so-and-so? Come up with a list of 10 characteristics. Then ask: What do you think so-and-so does when he's not [doing the thing in which he is most commonly observed]? The imaginary situation involving this character can be unusual, like having to deal with a stalking fan, but it can be perfectly ordinary, too, like a visit to his parents. We just want to see who this character is outside of his public role. Is he like his public self, or significantly different?

Once you and the writer have come up with a series of situations in which the character in question might be involved during his non-public hours, ask the writer to pick one and start elaborating. Remember the 5 Essentials, briefly recapped in this year's preface (plot, character, dialogue, setting, point of view):

- What's going to happen? (Plot)
- Who's involved? (Characters)
- Where is this taking place? (Setting)

And so on. Perhaps the best starting point, as with many short stories, is the situation. In what kind of situation are we going to observe this character?

Then, ask questions based on this situation. If so-and-so is visiting his parents:

- Is he going alone?
- Does he fly or drive?
- What happens when the airline doesn't have a record of his reservation?

Act as a kind of pitcher of story twists, lobbing new possibilities at the writer, who will have to figure out how the character would act. One of these "pitches" will result in a rich enough scenario that the writer will wish to focus on it for his assignment.

FICTION • WEEK 2 • MENTOR'S NOTES

Like last week, this exercise asks the writer to compose his answer as a scene rather than a series of bullet points or observations in narrative form. That means keeping a lot of balls in the air:

1. Coming up with a situation and characters
2. Deciding who's going to be telling the story (point of view)
3. Figuring out the proportions of show and tell

Start with the first challenge: **situation and characters.** As always, it helps to have a departure point. If the group in front at the supermarket has three people, two older and one younger, suggest the writer start with that detail. It seems like you're looking at two parents and a child. Ask: Where might they be going? Potential answers are:

- for ice cream
- their grandparents' house
- a friend's house for a slumber party
- boarding school

The answer the writer chooses will determine the next set of questions: If, say, it's "boarding school":

- Why are the parents packing the kid off to boarding school?
- Is he happy about it?
- Does he like it in his hometown?

Rely on your 5 Essentials and remember that effective mentoring means being ready for a make-your-own adventure type of process: The answer the writer chooses will determine the questions you should ask to prompt him for further clues to his material. Your constant support is the 5 Essentials: Every answer can be prompted for more information having to do with plot, character, dialogue, setting, and point of view.

Once the writer has a basic idea of what's going on and what kind of people he has on his hands – you might have him jot down some starter characteristics for each on a piece of paper (5 adjectives apiece) – you can start the conversation about how he wants to create the scene (**point of view** and **show vs. tell**):

Point of view:

- ☐ From the bird's eye view of an all-knowing narrator who's going to explain what's going on?
- ☐ From the more limited third-person perspective of a narrator stuck in the mind of one of the characters?
- ☐ First-person narrator?

Show vs. tell:

- ☐ Through unexplained dialogue between those in the car? (Pure showing)
- ☐ Through the author's presentation of actions, dialogue, etc? (Showing-through-telling)
- ☐ Through a mix?

Make sure the writer understands the distinctions between these forms of presentation. After reviewing the three examples in the lesson, ask him to restate their basic logic.

Last week's lesson combined character practice with a focus on show vs. tell. This week ups the ante by bringing in point of view. The previous level of this series concluded with the writer creating scenes that involve all 5 Essentials of traditional short fiction—plot, character, dialogue, setting, point of view. The last two week's exercises are working along the same lines, integrating various Essentials into simultaneous practice. The more advanced writer has to learn how to juggle them all at the same time.

Practicing writing against type is tricky because it inevitably brings up stereotypes, some of which are less innocent than others. Some are so odious that it's hardly necessary to write a short story demonstrating all the complexities and nuances of someone of a particular gender and race in order to disprove them. Stick with the more uncontroversial ones for this lesson, like what people tend to think of straight-A students (teachers' pets) or cowboys (rough-edged and reticent).

Start by having the student articulate the type. This may be uncomfortable, giving voice to narrow-minded views, but it's important for the student to realize in concrete terms what it is his job is to confront.

Then, ask questions. In what ways might this character depart from the cultural expectation? The easiest might be to start by enumerating the opposite characteristics. If cowboys are expected to be terse, maybe this one's a talker. If cowboys are expected to be stoic maybe this one's a hypochondriac. If they're expected to be chivalrous (there are positive stereotypes, too), this one can be a brawler.

The next step is to move away from this opposite extreme toward a more nuanced portrait of the character in question. A cowboy doesn't have to be terse, but he doesn't have to be an endless talker, either.

I remember traveling through Livingston, Montana, on a cross-country road trip. At a diner, I sat next to a man in paint-spattered coveralls, either fresh off a job or about to embark on one. In front of him, he had a plate of eggs through which he sliced as delicately as a high-society aristocrat. He ate slowly and deliberately. I asked him what he was reading. A book on parenting, he said. It made the argument that kids shouldn't be left to learn their life lessons from school peers, who are as clueless as they are. He said he had just finished *The Gulag Archipelago* by Aleksandr Solzhenitsyn, an epic, multi-volume book about forced-labor camp life in the Soviet Union. Then he went on to talk about his view that Solzhenitsyn was a reincarnation of one of the prophets of

Israel. Here in front of me was a housepainter with the eating habits of a French count, the reading interests of a careful father or a college graduate in Russian literature, and more than a passing interest in New Age spirituality. This man fit no type, either of a housepainter or of anyone else. And that is precisely why I remembered him vividly enough to write about him from memory right now. He's the epitome of a character against type. "Against type" may actually be the wrong designation here. He's not against type, or the opposite of type: he's *beside type*—an individual as eclectic and unique as most people are at core, and certainly as distinct and complex as every fiction character needs to be.

There are several steps in this exercise. The first is to figure out the situation. What kind of situation can pit two characters—forget for the moment how sympathetic or not they are—against each other? The writer has plenty of experience coming up with this kind of set-up from previous lessons.

The second is: What will make the reader sympathize with both characters in this situation? This doesn't demand anything very different from creating a single sympathizable character (though the writer may find the sympathetic qualities of the second referring back to the qualities of the first, as I did).

Discuss the things that make us like certain characters and dislike others. Discuss with the writer characters he has been reading about, and have him articulate *why* he likes certain ones and not others. You can do the same thing even for friends and acquaintances. What makes him like so-and-so? What about so-and-so? The writer can use these characteristics to draw his fictional characters.

The last challenge here is how to convey to the reader the likeability of these characters. Refer back to the trio of examples from last week. You can do it the way that I did it in this lesson: an all-knowing third-person narrator conveying the inner thoughts of both characters, but also presenting action (showing-and-telling). You can also do it though dialogue or narration of action without much explanation from an all-knowing narrator (showing). Or, you can do a mix of these. To keep the narrative moving, you can also tell us certain things straight out: "Sandra was nervous," as opposed to showing us her tying and re-tying her shoelaces, trying to get herself perfect for the big match.

Here's the challenge step-by-step:

1. Come up with a situation.
2. Come up with likeable characteristics ("L") for both characters.

3. Decide how you're going to convey those L's in terms of point of view and show vs. tell, as in Week 3.

This exercise ramps up a challenge the writer has already experienced: thinking closely about concrete vs. abstract word choice. The words in the assignment are purposefully tough to distinguish—not because the choice will be equally tough when writing a short story (if a writer is not sure how concrete a certain word sounds, he can just ditch it for a dozen others)—but to get the student to think very closely about words and what kind of imagery they conjure in a reader's mind.

Remind the student that concreteness and abstractness are not opposed states. Rather, they represent the end points of a spectrum. Something that's concrete in one sense is abstract in another (celebration, flowers, azaleas, etc.), so, it's often hard to say whether a word is abstract or concrete. Often, the answer is, simply, "It depends." Again, the ultimate idea here isn't to wrack our brains until we figure out the elusive either/or answer. It's to think hard and closely about the associations, feelings, and images created in a reader's mind by words.

The challenge exercise takes this idea further. It offers a familiar abstraction (love, sad, bitter, loud), but also less familiar ones. To "like" or "not like" something, is that concrete or abstract? In a short story? Quite abstract! A writer has to be more specific than "I don't like bitter foods." There are many ways to be more specific:

- "Bitter foods make me gag."
- "Bitter foods make me break out in scarlet welts."
- "When I was a boy, I overdosed on kale, so I can't touch bitter foods now."

These examples are all more concrete. Note that the first two discuss consequence, and the third discusses cause. But the first two sentences still suffer from abstraction –that "bitter foods" is quite undetailed. Can you, together with the writer, make this part of the sentence more concrete as well?

What else changes its look each day?

- Melting snow.
- The sun and moon (a little).
- The color of the sky. The sunset.
- The mood of a dog.

And so on. Feel free to recommend any of these to the writer. If she's having a hard time finding something to compare it to, step away from the exercise briefly and practice comparisons. Jot down several things and ask the student to compare them to something:

- When the cat snores, he sounds just like a ______.
- This apple is as green as a ________.
- The sun resembles the ________ of an egg.

This exercise is really no different from previous simile and metaphor exercises except that it asks the writer to keep going, keep digging to find new comparisons for the same thing, and to look ever more closely.

Here's a stab at a rewrite of the opening lines:

> I wish Kilroy wasn't such a shame at the table. When that boy starts ravaging his steak and beans, I get about as red as one of the sugarbeets I try to persuade him to eat once in a while: gristle flying, his snout flecked with grease, and his neighbor's dress shirt, too, if Kilroy's that kind of hungry. He's half the size of the dining table, so it's not like he's looking to listen.

The first sentence rephrases "had better manners" less literally: "wasn't such a shame." It makes a bigger, more visible change in the next sentence: "He eats so impolitely" is pure telling. A more vivid phrasing can bring this fact to life much more strikingly: "When that boy starts ravaging his steak..." Not "eating" his steak—*ravaging* his steak. Not "my face gets red," but "red as a sugarbeet I try..." (Note that the comparison stays in the food arena, for greater consistency. If I wrote as red as a traffic light, that would be okay, but a bit off-topic. And not only does it stay in the food arena, it finds a way to rope the comparison into the actual plot—not just "as red as a sugarbeet" but "as red as a sugarbeet *I try to persuade him to eat once in a while.*") The original keeps going, but my example pauses to animate the idea of bad manners even further: "Gristle flying, his snout flecked with grease..." Not "grease all over his *mouth*," but his *snout flecked* with grease." "Flecked" is more specific and concrete than "all over" because it signifies droplets; and "snout" is certainly more concrete than mouth, while continuing to keep alive the suggestion that this is a boy, not a dog. (If a human is chowing down in a particularly animalistic way, one way to convey that is to refer to his mouth as that of an animal.) The next sentence keeps after the specifics: not "he's a big guy" but "he's half the size of the dining table."

Certain things in the original are as specific as can be: chicken bone, broom, conscientious objector (if the writer doesn't know what that is, ask her to look it up online), judo, head lock, blouse, bawling, etc. And Mr. Halbert's speech is pretty distinctive ("real regretful"). But there are just as many opportunities for greater concreteness ("snorted" instead of "laughed"), comparison (Kilroy kicked Pete, which set Pete *yowling like a house alarm*"), vividness through word choice ("Mr. Halbert wouldn't curse a thief" instead of "doesn't believe in conflict") and synonyms ("huffed" instead of "tried to get his breath back"), and so on.

"Technical" language often overlaps with simply specific language, and isn't an indiscriminately positive device. Having too many technical terms can freeze the reader out of a story because he or she can't understand half of what's in it, and isn't the kind of reader to go looking up every unfamiliar term. That said, technical language *can* bring a tremendous feeling of authenticity to a story, the sense that the world being described is "real," not invented, which is the illusion that every writer of fiction seeks.

There is no straightforward, formulaic way to do "research." Hanging around a mechanics' shop is about as effective as research gets. That is, hanging around is usually much more effective, in a roundabout way, than dutifully making notes from the encyclopedia or a how-to book in a library. It's also a lot more fun. When I decided that my novel should have a section set in New Orleans, I moved there for a month and tried to soak up as much of the way locals spoke and lived as I could. It got me a whole lot more than reading every book written about New Orleans, though I did that, too. "Hanging around" is likely to suggest many more scene ideas, also.

Some writers might disparage the idea of "research," but I think what they mean is that they frown on the idea of research showing through in the story. If a character is spouting an encyclopedic selection of facts about his or her subculture, that's going to be dry and not very believable. Our dentist wouldn't be lecturing Mandy on what a scap drill is because she would know. (For instance, when I needed to supply the reader with some information like this—called **exposition**—in my novel, I had one character say it to another who was visiting New Orleans for the first time. So there was a reason *inside the narrative* for exposition of this kind.)

This is why I suggested the writer root around for several hours, whether online, in a book, or by hanging around, and then set the notes aside as she works on her fragment. Specialists of many kinds (skiers, wrestlers, etc.) talk about learning and practicing as much as possible before the competition, but then letting go of all that rational preparation when the contest begins and relying on instinct instead. They're not completely starting from scratch, but they're not hobbled by overthinking the facts, either. This roughly resembles what I'm proposing here. Research involves filling up with information and then discarding it. The writer can peek back if she knows what term she needs but has simply forgotten the word, but she shouldn't be dutifully trying to plug in as many technical words as she can.

Dialect has continuity with ordinary dialogue. Dialect may be specific to time and place, but there's almost no place that speaks *without* dialect. Even British English is a dialect.

The big challenge—and perhaps the most fun—of this assignment is figuring out how to spell English words in dialect, and render mispronounced words. Here's an example of a grammatical English sentence rendered in a Russian-American accent and in a plummy British dialect:

American: Darling, I don't presume to know everything, but do wear that parka—it's so cold outside.

Russian-American: Darling, I don't prezoom to know evorytyng, but do wear zat parka—it's saw colt outsight.

British: Dahling, I don't prezyoom to know avvvvvrahthing, but do weah that pahka —it's so kah-old outside.

Now, these three speakers wouldn't only pronounce the same words differently. They'd also make the same point using different words.

British: Dahling, I don't prezyoom to know avvvvvrahthing, but do weah that pahka —it's so kah-old outside.

Russian-American: I don't know evorytyng, but wear ze coat, okay? It's rilly colt outsight.

American: I don't know everything, but I know it's freezing out there. Better put on that parka.

You might help the writer by isolating how concision works. Ask:

1. Is there redundant information?
2. Is there superfluous information?
3. Can certain things be implied by others and not have to be stated outright?
4. Can sentences be consolidated?
5. Can information be conveyed later (or earlier) using less language?

Practice by taking out certain words or phrases. Ask the writer:

1. Has this changed the meaning?
2. Does the reader still know everything she needs to know?
3. If not, is there a way to put the information back in using fewer words?

Finally, if the writer's doing the second challenge assignment, talk about voice:

1. How would you describe the speaking style of this character?
2. Based on his or her voice, let's create a character portrait of this individual.
3. Let's practice saying other things in this character's voice.

In general, **make concision a priority in the writer's work from now on**, even when it isn't an explicit assignment in the lesson. The challenge with advanced writing is to keep lots of balls in the air at once, making sure that one's work is vivid, concise, technically precise, and so on, all at the same time.

Finally, here's my concise version of the second paragraph about Rich and his dad:

> I need Rich because my eyes don't see too well. Rich isn't too easy on the go himself. If I'm blind, he's fat. Barely fits behind the wheel of his car. He's my

> son, so I love him no matter what, and last time I checked, Wal-Mart doesn't deliver warm coats. When I hang up, I move to the living room windows, so I can hear the bell. Because the thing is—I can't hear too well, either.

82 words vs. the original's 121. I saved $39! I can buy a very fancy steak.

You'll notice I left a little bit more here than in the first paragraph. Technically, we could have replaced "my eyes" with "I" in the first sentence, and we could have changed "too well" to, simply, "well." But as I've discussed, a story isn't only a dump of information; voice matters as well. And there's something about this man's way of speech that brings him alive. All those times he tells us that it's "his son Rich" he's talking about; however, we know it's his son by this point and can cut that out. And we don't need him to tell us someone has to "come up on the steps" in order to ring the bell.

There are other particularities of speech—the fact that he prefaces "so I love him no matter what" with "he's my son..."; the humor of "And last time I checked"—that maybe we ought to keep in our first draft. I say *maybe* because concision isn't a science. In fact, what we have here is a simulation of what authors go through with their characters all the time: What to keep? What to throw out? What sounds silly? What sounds authentic?

So here's what my concise version of the two paragraphs looks like, at 119 words, compared to the original's 221.

> The winter came without warning. In one day, the temperature dropped forty degrees and it started to snow. My jacket wasn't worth much, so I called Rich: "Son, we have to drive down to the box store."
>
> I need Rich because my eyes can't see too well. Rich isn't too easy on the go himself. If I'm blind, he's fat. Barely fits behind the wheel of his car. He's my son, so I love him no matter what, and last time I checked, Wal-Mart doesn't deliver warm coats. When I hang up, I move to the bay windows in the living room, so I can hear the bell. Because the thing is—I can't hear too well, either.

Here are some sample answers:

1. Stanley was lazy.

   "Stanley rolled over to peek at the alarm clock. Noon. One more hour, he decided." [**action**]

2. Beverly was pretty.

   "I swear, if one more boy comes knocking on this door!" Beverly's father shouted to no one in particular. "She has to focus on school!" [**speech**]

3. The weather had turned bad.

   "The sky, clear just moments before, had turned a gleaming, vicious silver." [A trick answer, because it's still told, just with a lot more animating detail, and without the words "the weather turned bad" being used.]

4. They had never met.

   "He scanned the crowd, then threw up his hands. How in the world was he supposed to know what she looked like?" [**thoughts**]

5. Overcast skies always made him depressed.

   "The sky, clear just moments before, had turned a vicious, gleaming silver. Stanley, who had been about to rise, closed his eyes again, and decided, One more hour." [**action** and **thought**]

6. John couldn't eat fruit.

   "After I came home, I threw up for hours!"

   "Well, sir, why are you certain it was the restaurant's fault?"

   "Maybe it wasn't, but I need to know what was in that steak sauce. I have allergies."

   "The steak sauce? I'm afraid that's a trade secret, sir."

   "Just tell me, does it have fruit?"

"A touch of blueberry, yes."

"Fruit? In the steak sauce? I am going to sue!" [**dialogue**]

7. In this community, no secret stayed that way for long.

   "Barbara Howell had heard that the Pitkins woman was pregnant with triplets almost as soon as Mrs. Pitkins knew it herself." [Like #3, **showing-as-telling.**]

8. Randy Brown had a big ranch.

   "First thing Randy Brown did every morning was stand astride the bed of his truck and gaze out at his property. Even on the clearest day, he couldn't see the end of it, and he liked that a whole lot." [**action** and **thought**]

9. He was a pacifist.

   "'Make muffins, not war,' a button on his jacket said." [**appearance**]

10. The trees had been planted by his grandfather.

    This one is a trick. As the writer will hopefully see after trying to show this information, this information is best told, plainly and directly.

There's plentiful guidance in the lesson, but it's fairly advanced. Keep the writer anchored by reminding him of what could be described as the three basic approaches to show and tell:

> **Tell**: She was sad.
> **Show**: She had gone through one box of tissues and was starting in on another.
> **Tell-and-show**: She was so sad, she was starting in on a second box of tissues.

Telling is the more frequent resort of nonfiction. It's essayistic, explanatory, analytical. Showing could be described as exemplifying the information in the told variant, without revealing it directly. Perhaps it would help the writer to compare it to charades. A mime of tears coming from eyes will invariably result in someone screaming out "sad!" In the same way, if you ask someone, What would you say about someone who "had gone through one box of tissues and was starting in on another?" Chances are you'll hear the answer: "She's sad." So, showing is to the mimed part of charades as telling is to the accurate-answer part.

By this point, the starting point in this kind of exercise should seem familiar to the writer:

- Come up with a situation.
- Think about point of view.
- Figure out how the story will open.
- Write it without thinking about show and tell, if that helps.

Only then should the writer give conscious thought to how he can rephrase the opening 500 words more effectively through show-and-tell. That's the purpose of this exercise, at least. In the future, when his instinct is more developed, it will be something he thinks about intuitively, as part of story planning.

Figuring out when to tell and when to show is a delicate, subtle art that takes years to develop. Encourage the writer to have fun and not worry about getting it just right this time. Getting a handle on the distinctions between the three approaches above would be a great start for now.

Act as a guinea pig in this exercise: Read the writer's authenticating sentences and quickly answer: do they put you right there? Rope in other family members for the same test.

Here are sample answers to some of the remaining entries:

Objects

Jeans:

> "'Gene's Jeans,' that's your idea?" Corey snorted. "Please say you're joking."
>
> Gene looked around the warehouse, jeans in every fit and size looming above them like an acid-washed mountain. "Jeans in your Genes?" he shrugged.
>
> "You're such a cornball," Corey said.

Explanation: Very often, the best way to authenticate isn't by describing something directly. If I'd dutifully described the appearance of the jeans, the description may have been detailed and concrete enough to persuade you. (And I do do that a little bit with the "acid-washed mountain.") But instead I focused on the two friends debating what to name the place. It's a trick authentication: Of course the jeans are there and real, even though I don't describe them in detail. Why else would these two people be arguing abut what to name the store?

Ice-cream truck:

> "The generator had given out, so Mr. Paulson switched off the musical tinkle, which drove him mad, anyway, and raced around Pond Park, booming through his megaphone—"Melting ice cream for half the price, melting ice cream for half the price!"—as the truck left a trail

of vanilla and chocolate on the baking pavement. He cleared out his inventory for the first time all summer, and went home three hours early."

Explanation: This is a looooong sentence. (Next year, the writer and I will be practicing the virtuoso task of composing a very long sentence with many clauses.) There are quite a few authenticating details here: The generator's broken down; it turns out Mr. Paulson hates the music that he's forced to play when the truck is working fine, so he's half-relieved; the truck leaves a trail of vanilla and chocolate on the pavement, not something that happens customarily. But the best part is that the disaster turns out to be an unexpected blessing for Mr. Paulson. That's the most authenticating detail of all.

Characters

A woman named Christina:

"Christina," she introduced herself. "Go by Chri."
"Cree? Like the tribe?" Professor Tambor said.
"No, Chri." She spelled it.
"By Golly, girl," Tambor said, screwing up his eyebrows. "Your name has more nicknames than any out there – Kristin, Christy, Chris – and you go by Chri?"
"Exactly," she said. "Gotta stand out somehow."

Explanation: Do you doubt this woman is named Christina?

Circus clown:

"This is the last time I'm having this conversation with you, the last time!" Rick rasped into the phone as he wedged a clown's nose on the considerable bulb of the one nature (or, more accurately, his plump momma) had given him. Showtime was in three minutes. "I've gone three years without a raise, Riggs," he yelled into the phone.
"Three years! You bump me up in the new contract or I'm off to Barnum and Bailey, mark my words."

Explanation: Some people think of clowns as happy, some as sad, but I think few of us remember that they're businesspeople too. That's the authenticating detail here.

Places

Highway:

> "Out here, highways follow river valleys, my friend. Rail lines. They don't light off into the prairie for no good reason. I'm telling you: We're lost."

Explanation: Research/technical know-how.

Bandstand:

> "Whoever had built the bandstand must have had an odd notion of acoustics: It was walled in with baroquely fretted ironwork on three sides. All the same, a band in full mariachi gear piled in every sunset and blew its horns at the crowd."

Explanation: This bandstand doesn't make much sense. And that's exactly why it's real.

Remind the writer to not worry about memorizing the terms so much as understanding the logic behind the various points of view. Try to sensitize the writer to the way every fictional form takes some kind of point of view by asking her to discuss it when you're reading a book or watching a television show, film, or play.

If the writer gets stuck, ask her to use my examples as guidelines. Always start with the three questions:

- Who's telling the story?
- How much does s/he know?
- Is s/he a part of the story?
- To whom is s/he telling it?

To do the challenge exercise, the writer will have to come up with a handful of situations. If he's struggling, he can use the same one for each of the examples. In fact, that's a good exercise, too.

After coming up with a situation, is it possible to tell what kind of point of view would be best for it? It often is, but it's hard to teach because it's the work of instinct, the ground shifting in every case. We'll practice it more next year. For now, help the writer come up with a situation and find a way to demonstrate the POV in the text of the example.

As the writer is working on the scene, encourage him or her to do several drafts. The first one is likely to be awkward, concerned mostly with setting down some key details. That having been done, the second is likely to give the writer the mental space to experiment with telling some details and showing others.

The other critical element here is to justify to the writer the value of climbing inside foreign minds. It's a tricky thing, to get inside the mind of someone unlike us, especially if it's a person we disagree with. More often than not, we human beings handle this kind of divergence by not thinking about it, because conflict is unpleasant. A fiction writer can't afford to do that. That doesn't mean she has to muck around in nastiness. Think of it as an opportunity. A flattering portrait of Gandhi is probably going to be less affecting than the kind of portrait we saw of the Nazi officer Amon Goeth by the actor Ralph Fiennes in Steven Spielberg's *Schindler's List*. Make no mistake: Goeth is evil, and no one walks away from the film admiring him. But he would have been a boring, hackneyed character had he been caricaturishly evil. Even evil has to be represented with skill and nuance. Because even evil has its own position, vile as it may be. Fiction doesn't pretty up that position, but it does have to represent it without stereotype and reduction. That sort of simplistic telling harms the fiction, not the evil character it's meant to abuse.

For someone of high-school age, this is a sensitive topic, and guidance from a mentor is especially critical. That's why your involvement, as much intellectually and philosophically as craft-related, is critical in this lesson.

The two parts of this exercise are to create a character profile and write a scene from that person's point of view. Here are some questions and prompts to get the writer's mind stirring in both parts:

Character profile:

1. Write a diary entry from this person's point of view.

2. Take us through a day in this person's life, from morning to night.
3. Give us 10 things that she or he thinks about. Stay away from typecasting thoughts, like boys and football or girls and cooking.
4. Imagine this person talking to a friend, talking to a parent.
5. What makes this person laugh? Cry?
6. What does this person dream about?
7. What are this person's pet peeves?
8. Imagine a debate between yourself and this person.
9. Imagine this person in three situations in which you've never observed him or her directly.
10. Imagine this person doing a character profile of you.

Scene:

1. Are you going to do a scene that concerns your relationship to this person directly? Or are you going to simply show this person in his or her element?
2. Are you simply going to show this person in his or her element, without much explanation – remember, it's a scene, so you don't have to worry about suspense, conflict, quest, etc. – or have some tell, or show-and-tell, about what this person is like?
3. Either way, probably some portion of the scene will have to be shown, so what aspect of the character profile would you like to focus on? What in your column makes you the most interested or curious about the person you're imagining?

In this lesson, your greatest contribution, once again, will be moral and intellectual rather than craft-related. The writer knows the basics. What he needs help with here is understanding the concept of untested ideas, and the related question of why fiction is such a good tool for exploring them.

The writer may be more inclined to start by exploring in more detail a positive unknown, like a curiosity. That's fine: In some ways, it's as emotionally challenging an assignment as the opposite because it entails complicating one's positive impression by finding the subject's risks, challenges, and drawbacks. In turn, testing out a prejudice, dislike, anger, fear, or anxiety is about trying to find in its source the kinds of redeeming qualities that may soften the negativity of the feeling.

Either way, fiction is an ideal tool here because, in its essence, it demands specificity and detail. Prejudices and fears are convenient because they weed out conflicting detail, as even my positive curiosity about the American West did. This exercise makes that kind of evasion impossible.

What's the purpose of doing an exercise like this, you might ask. It *is* a departure for the syllabus because apart from practicing craft, it uses craft to improve something that might be called **ways of seeing**. A fiction writer is more than her craft toolbox. Just as much depends on her sensibility, the way she perceives things. Writers are hardly model human beings – Ezra Pound was an anti-Semite; Ernest Hemingway killed himself; F. Scott Fitzgerald drank himself to death. But these are not job requirements (though our culture sometimes romanticizes them foolishly). Neither is niceness nor wholesomeness. In fact, it's as problematic as prejudice or brutality. The world isn't always nice or wholesome, and any fiction that represents it as such is naïve and does the reader a disservice. Rather, the writer's job is to appreciate complexity, to render the world in all its nuance, just like one of those Rembrandt paintings whose quality of darkness seems to include a thousand colors. The best writer needs to see the magic in ugliness, and the ugliness in beauty. *That* is the point of this exercise. The writer can never settle for a distant idea of something, be it idealized or brutally real.

Do you remember the exercise from late last year that asked the writer to change up the five dominant elements (plot, character, dialogue, point of view, setting) in a story situation and scene with which he had come up? That was revision by another name.

It may be productive to revisit that exercise. This week's assignment isn't asking for something very different, so it would make a good confidence-builder, reminding the writer that he already has experience with this.

Otherwise, start by asking the writer to reread what he wrote last week. If he finished it only a day or two before, wait several days before starting this assignment.

Start with a debrief:

1. What in this story worked well?

2. What didn't?

3. Go through the 5 Essentials:

    a. Is the plot solid? Are there any holes? Does it use conflict, quest, or suspense as effectively as it can?

    b. Who are the characters? Maybe you need one more, or you should cut one out?

    c. Do they speak? Is it stilted? Maybe make another run through the dialogue? Maybe introduce dialogue, if none yet exists?

    d. Who's telling the story? Are you discovering this approach to be limiting in any way?

    e. Where are we? Does it need to be fleshed out in more detail?

Remember that we're dealing with an opening here, so while the answer to these questions might be yes, it also might be something best done later in the story. If all this means the writer would get better revision practice by writing a scene rather than the opening, that's fine.

After asking the writer these questions, give him your own impressions. To make things more interesting, you might want to play the role of a Hollywood studio head who's reviewing the opening for its potential as the start of a film script. The suggestions such a person would give to the script writer are called "notes." If the writer is struggling to come up with his own ideas for revision, give the writer some "notes."

One other option is for the writer to do #3 above: simply rewrite the opening from scratch. Even if he's trying to replicate the details exactly (don't let him look at the original more than once), he's going to end up with something different and invariably better: The Sensei Rule in effect.

FICTION • WEEK 18 • MENTOR'S NOTES

As in earlier levels of this course, don't supervise the writer's work this week except in broad terms: Make sure she fulfills the assignment, and discuss any questions or concerns she may have. Let her drive the discussion this week. Volunteer to read the story, and offer observations and suggestions, but start by inviting the writer to talk about

- What she thinks she did well in the story;
- What less so;
- How she thinks she might be able to improve it in a revision;
- What it made her realize, if anything, about the subject matter.

Because the mentor usually drives the discussion, the writer may be overly accustomed to the idea that the editorial observation must come from you. Change that this week. Both you and the writer may be surprised by the strong feelings, impressions, and questions the writer may be carrying about the experience. In fact, this kind of writer-driven debrief should become a regular part of your mentoring work with her as we advance to the final level of this series.

Other questions with which to prompt the writer:

1. Did you try anything new in this story?
2. Did you find yourself doing something better because you'd practiced it before?
3. What was difficult?
4. Do you like the story? How would you rate it on a scale of 1-10? What's your favorite part of the story?
5. Let's draw a table featuring the subjects of all the lessons this year. Next to them, give yourself a 1-10 rating on how well you think you did on them in this week's story.
6. Did this story give you any ideas for other stories?

7. Can you say, in 25 words or less, what this story is about, what the story idea/situation are?
8. Can you do the same for each of the characters?
9. Who's telling the story? Is this a first or third-person narrator? How much does he or she know about what the characters are feeling and thinking? To whom is this narrator telling the story?
10. Did you think about each of the 5 Essentials? (Plot, character, dialogue, point of view, setting.) Can you tell in what order? If you had to re-set the story, where would you set it?

More broadly:

1. Which lesson or section this year was the most interesting for you? Least interesting? Most confusing?
2. What would you like to practice most next year?
3. Can you describe how your understanding of creative writing has changed since you started the first level of this series, if you've been using it since then?
4. If somebody asked for your help in writing a short story, what would you tell them?
5. Has your practice of writing led you to different conclusions than what this syllabus has taught? (This would be absolutely fine.)

The lesson features fairly detailed directions, so here I just want to focus for a little bit longer on the notion of working with an existing poem. I'm sure no poet loves the idea of her poem being rewritten by anyone else. I wouldn't. Once, I tried to condense a short story that I wanted to use in an anthology I was editing, but the author refused me, and rightfully so.

But that was for publication. For private practice, we'll hope that Sharon Olds will forgive us for wanting to experiment with "Feared Drowned." I see it as a testament to the poem's quality and richness. Besides, when a poet publishes her poem, she releases it into the world, and relinquishes some rights over it. In a sense, it becomes ours as much as hers. We acquire the right to define it for ourselves.

For a young writer, nothing helps as much as tinkering with a published poem. It persuades him in subtle ways that art is not a finished, monolithic thing, flawless and of only one meaning, known in full only to the author and to be divined by the audience. It helps the young writer understand that there are many ways to write a poem, and this is only one outcome. It helps the writer by giving him a base from which to imagine what the poem *doesn't* look like—as I explain in this lesson and throughout this book, imagining what *isn't* there is often a great way to understand better what *is* and why—a base that isn't available if the writer is staring at a blank page.

One of the most significant aspects of comparison is *dominant detail.* To use a hoary old cliché, you want to be comparing apples to apples.

For instance, in "your bearded head slick as a ____________," the dominant details are roundedness (head), furriness (beard), and wetness (slick). The dominant one among the dominants is slickness, since the simile is "slick as a..." (A good side exercise here is to ask the writer: Is "slick as a..." a simile or comparison?) The roundedness is probably next in importance, since the comparison makes us think of a round head, wet with water, emerging from the deep. "Bearded" seems primarily a modifier here.

Options:

- ...your bearded head slick as an eel (Not great, because it doesn't invoke the roundedness.)
- ...your bearded head slick as moss (Better – moss is kind of soft-edged, furry, and often damp.)
- ...your bearded head slick as a puddle (Again, so-so, because puddles hardly have a furry appearance, but they do have roundish shapes, and are certainly slick, and carry a connotation of loss for me. Comparisons don't stand alone; they have to communicate with the content around them, so isolating them like this doesn't help. Make sure the writer remembers that in this first stanza, the subject is rising worry, loss, anxiety. In another context, "puddle" may not have been so great, but here, it feeds into the subject of the poem.)

It's going to be very tough for the writer to find alternatives that evoke so many associations. Simply have her aim for as many as possible; it's a great brain-teaser and skill-improver, even if she couldn't find an alternative that evokes every last association.

The rest of the comparisons:

3. clutching the towel like ____________ (The writer can compare the clutching or, like Olds does, the towel. Remember the surrounding content here: That same worry and fear.)

4. Rocks stick out near the shore like ____________ (The comparison here rests pretty squarely on the shape of the rocks.)

5. Kelp snakes in like ____________ (The dominant detail here is squiggliness, though also color, the brown-green of kelp.)

6. his beard matted like ____________ (The dominant detail is mattedness, tangledness, furriness, though color—the brown/black of a beard – is relevant, too.)

7. his suit dark as ____________ (This one is very broad. Darkness is the dominant detail, though the shape of the swimming suit, as discussed, is relevant, too.)

You'll notice all these are similes. In this poem, Olds seems much fonder of them than metaphors. There's something grand, and grandly confident, about metaphors. Similes are more tentative, more timid—they don't make claims as large as "X is actually Y," merely "X reminds us of Y." That, too, goes with the content of the poem—the narrator has been frightened, and is in no mood to make confident pronouncements about the state of things in the world.

The writer's reorganization can be random to start. But then, he should try to rewrite the poem with reason in mind, as I tried to do. This will force him to think about why Sharon Olds has broken up her stanzas where she has. We may not be able to arrive at an answer, but trying to find one is the point.

Why does Sharon Olds end each stanza with a complete sentence? What does that full rest evoke? Doesn't this, too, contradict the roiling, rushing chaos of the narrator's emotions? Perhaps it's countered by the rush of the lines that precede the last line in each stanza, few of which end on a period.

With what does each stanza concern itself? The first announces the narrator's fear; the second deals with her attempts to find her missing husband; the third describes what she sees; the fourth paces in place by restating that she can't find him. The fifth conveys her response, and the final one her takeaway from the experience. So, almost every stanza describes a new part of the experience. (Not all poems proceed in this almost story-like way, which is why I wanted the writer to start by unpacking something more accessible, like this poem.) I'm not saying this explanation is right. Sharon Olds would probably disagree, which makes me no less correct—and your writer is equally entitled, not to say obligated, to come up with his own explanation.

A note about *thinking* about how to reorganize vs. using *instinct*:

A rational logic can guide the writer in his reorganization, based on what he thinks the poem is trying to say. Or he can reorganize based on instinct, finding words for the motivation later.

There's a fine line between following the subtle call of instinct and simply being random —especially if the writer can't articulate *why* it feels right to split up lines x and y. But the writer has been honing his instinct for a couple of years now, and it may be worth trusting it. Not everything, ultimately, needs to be articulated. Being able to analyze one's work is far less important than being able to create good work.

Many of the best writers are surprised by critical analyses of their work—they reveal something to the writer as much as to the audience. How could this be, you might wonder. Didn't this person think about what he was doing? He did; he thought about it a lot. But then, as with the research lesson in the fiction section, he let all his preparation go, and asked himself what felt right. It's a subtle talent, something that even the most advanced writers often lack. It's necessary to learn what I'm teaching here, but it's just as necessary at key moments, having learned it, to let go of our rote knowledge of it, and just trust instinct.

This exercise may be one time to practice that with the writer. If he can't intellectually justify his reorganization in a neat, form-relates-to-content way, that's fine. If the new order "feels right," but he can't say why, that's ok. You may try to put words to it together, or you can simply leave the product alone. Not everything about our artistic motivations needs to be dissected and analyzed.

As Mary Oliver points out, how a line ends is the most important thing about it. Ending it on a complete sentence is natural to our ears because a period signifies an end. For the same reason, ending it in the middle of a sentence is disruptive, forcing us to pay a heightened kind of attention. Perhaps it's an uncomfortable attention because we are having to hold line 1 in our minds as we rush along to line 2. (Many poems ask you to go on to lines 3 and 4 and beyond before things start to cohere.) But you'll agree that your senses are more alert than they are with an *end-stopped* line (Line that ends with a piece of terminal punctuation: period, question mark, or exclamation mark.)

The best thing you can do for this exercise is to help the writer begin to grasp just how many possibilities line endings give a poet, and how consequential her choices in this department can be. Imagine a poem full of short lines, with one very long one. Doesn't that one long line draw more attention than if it had appeared in a poem of long lines? Varying line length in this way allows a poet to point a big arrow at the one that stands out without inserting overly obvious language in that line. ("This is important!") Starting a line not flush with the left-hand margin in a poem of otherwise left-justified lines has the same effect. In the poems you and the writer consider this week, take a microscope to the shape of the line:

- where it begins
- how it's punctuated
- where it ends
- how that compares to the same answers for the rest of the poem's lines
- how these answers interact with what the poem seems to be about

The difference between two versions of the same poem whose lines are broken in different ways is extremely subtle and subjective. If the writer is struggling to put words to how the two versions are different, ask the following questions:

1. Which version moves faster? Does this agree with what you think the poem is about?

2. Which version has more energy? Why?

3. Which version is easier to read?

4. As the first version is read to you, write down three images that come to mind. Do the same for the second version.

5. Read both versions, with the appropriate pauses, to a young sibling, if you have one. Which one is easier to understand?

Of course, sound associations go far beyond "hard" and "soft," but grasping that basic distinction is sufficient for now. A great way to drive home the difference in hard vs. soft sounds—and practice finding synonyms while you're at it—is to ask the writer to come up with several pairs of synonyms, and then evaluate the different imagery those words bring up because of their sounds, as Mary Oliver does with "rock" vs. "stone." (Rock is sharp-angled—*r, k*—and stone, despite the hardness of that *t*, is softened by the vowel with which it ends.)

To use our standbys since page 1 of Year 1 ("throw," "chuck," and "lob"):

- "Chuck" is clearly the hardest of the three: *Ch, ck.* The meaning corresponds, doesn't it? (To throw with derision or carelessness.)
- "Throw" is gentler, less rough than "chuck," though less arcing than "lob." (You could say "throw" has more of an arc than "chuck" and less of one than "lob," time in the air being a kind of signifier of gentleness.) That hard *t* is softened by the *h*, and the *r*, in turn, is softened by the *ow*.
- "Lob" is a tricky one. *B* is as hard a sound as they come, with *l* able to go either way. (The *l* in both "pal" and "lob" is pretty hard, even though one is at the beginning and one at the end. The *l* in "pale" is very soft thanks to that concluding *e,* as is the *l* in "slurry" because it follows the whispering, soft "s." It all depends.) If "lob" meant "chuck," I, for one, wouldn't be surprised. But in another sense, the letters mimic the meaning of the word: *L* is the firm hand that sends the ball flying, *o* its long arc, and *b* the hard landing that it makes when it comes back down.

Here's another way to familiarize the writer with sound and how we instinctively choose different words depending on the mood we're in or the effects we intend to conjure. Ask her to perform the following experiment: In the course of a week, pick a designated daily time at which she will, in her notebook, describe her mood.

When the seven days are up, review the log with the writer. Obviously, she will have chosen words whose *meaning* accurately reflects her mood. But my argument is that their *sound* will be a reflection of her mood as well—perhaps in a different way than their meaning.

The ultimate purpose of this exercise is for the writer to experience a broader range of rhyme-derived rhythms than she did in previous levels of this syllabus.

She can impose a rhyme scheme on "Feared Drowned" randomly, or she might think about the content of the poem, and come up with a rhyme scheme that speaks to it. For instance, the poem is about fear and disorientation. Does that mean it can't have any patterning, such as rhyme? No. That just means it needs to be subtle. So, why not a rhyme scheme without order: the first line in Stanza 1 rhymes with the third in Stanza 2, then with the second in Stanza 3, and so on.

If that's too complicated a challenge, the writer can start the same way she did last year: by writing out the last words of each line, coming up with a handful of rhymes for each, then seeing which might work in the context of the poem without too much awkwardness.

The second challenge exercise asks her to do the assignment in reverse: undo rhymes, replacing them with synonyms that leave the meaning intact. (A good synonym exercise, too.) Debrief the writer after she has finished about the aural impact of the two versions:

1. Which do you prefer? Why?
2. Jot down the first three associations that come to mind as I read the two versions aloud to you.
3. Imagine each set to music. What music genre would each be?
4. What do you like best and least about each version?
5. If you had to attend a poetry reading, in what kind of venue would one be read and in what kind the other?

As with any poem, beginning is the toughest thing. So? Don't begin. Poems don't have to begin at the beginning, at least during the first draft.

First, ask the writer to settle on a subject. The first challenge exercise may actually serve as a worthwhile precursor to the main exercise. After he has chosen one, ask him to brainstorm images, associations, words, etc. In fact, he can draw a series of columns, filling each with words, images, scenes, etc. that the subject conjures for him and that he may wish to include in the poem.

Very often, brainstorming in this way will detour me to the composition of a stanza. That stanza may not end up as the first one, but riffing in this way is a great way to feel around for the entry point of a poem. It's also less daunting than staring at a blank page, figuring out how something should begin.

Once the writer has completed a single stanza, it may recommend another, or make clear that something else needs to come before it. He may choose to "show" by describing a situation that clearly deals with a fear, even if that word never appears, the way Sharon Olds does, or issue a set of direct observations about a specific fear, the way John Keats and Shakespeare do. Note that Olds' method is a lot more modern. There's a lot more "telling," speaking broadly, in older poetry, when poets had a lot more cultural authority to pronounce on the way things were and weren't.

Even if the writer's instincts about word choice, line breaks, etc. aren't perfectly honed, he should by no means overthink these decisions. Let the things he's learned about in this unit sit in the back of his mind, but he should by no means plan to have stanzas of x many lines. The first step is to spit up the images and ideas brought up by the subject. It is only during revision, the bulk of the content set down, that the writer should begin to play with the other tools at his disposal. (More on revision next year.) If the writer sets himself craft tasks—the number of lines in the poem's stanzas, patterns in line breaks, recurring imagery—before he's figured out what the poem's about, he will be starting with the last thing first.

If the student is struggling to come up with a poem from scratch, there are lots of modified ways to do the exercise. Pick a poem that she loves. Read it together and underline every comparison, just as we did in the "Feared Drowned" unit. Then, find a new comparison for each of the comparisons in the poem.

If there are no comparisons in the poem, come up with a handful.

This would work well with a poem or poem fragment the writer may have written herself.

This lesson is meant to be fun, a bit of game-playing after the intense unit that started us off this year. However, its playfulness is deceptive. There are few lessons in the past three years that pack as much of a wallop, craft-wise. A one-line poem is to a standard poem as a short story is to a novel: it has that much less room in which to work its magic. Its words ring that much more loudly, and, therefore, have to be chosen that much more carefully. It has that much less room to say everything it wants to say, and, as a result has to say that much by the silence that follows, the way Ernest Hemingway's harrowing six-line "story" does.

Hemingway's "story" was an inspiration for what might be called the "Six-word memoir project," a running feature of a magazine called *SMITH*, which asked users to post whatever's on their mind in six words or less. (This is a variation on social-networking services like Twitter which limit contributions to 140 characters. But it's a big variation because 140 characters is quite loose compared to six words.) Together with the writer —but you first, since not all the entries are appropriate—review some of the six-word memoirs at http://www.smithmag.net/sixwords/. Better yet, visit the library and have a look at *Not Quite What I Was Planning,* the book *SMITH* magazine published of some of the best six-word memoirs, featuring both famous and unknown authors. As one reviewer of the book's sequel wrote, "Six words. Personal stories. Infinite possibilities."

In helping the writer come up with a one-line poem of her own, look around: Look at advertising slogans, taglines, street signs, announcements in store windows. Many things can become poetry if reduced to the length of a single line. The bagginess of a paragraph is almost irreconcilable with poetry, but given no more than a single line, even the pedestrian tagline of a TV commercial for an SUV allowed to echo out into nothingness—"The SUV is back"—gains an eerie impact.

The key here is to isolate what it is about, say, "1861" that reads and feels more obviously "poetic" than "Mending Wall." It's a subjective and abstract task, one with no final answer, necessarily, but it would help to make a list with the writer:

1. Take Line 3. "Not you..." the poet says. But what is he responding to? We don't know. He's dwelling on the appropriate description for such a turbulent year, but he doesn't say "I wouldn't describe you..."; he launches right into it, as if responding to an off-stage conversation or happenstance. This poem is less concerned with context than the Frost poem.

2. The poem proceeds by avalanching description ("But as a strong man, erect, clothed in blue clothes, advancing, carrying a rifle on your shoulder..."—five descriptive clauses in that pair of lines alone) that shifts to other scenes of description rather than by the traditional prose sequence of noun-verb, noun-verb, etc.

3. The poem isn't telling a "story" so much as issuing a series of exclamations. The heightened tone (and diction, too) identifies this as poetic territory as well.

4. The language is elevated and baroque: "poetling," "round-lipp'd." Frost's language is hardly plain as well ("where they have left not one stone on a stone") but in the service of more traditional syntax.

5. Overall, Whitman's poem is more fragmented, more charged, more jagged than traditional prose.

Although I gave the student an example of my work on Part 1, I did not provide my own work on Part 2. I include it here so that you may make use of it to help the student out.

The opening paragraphs of "The Golden Goose" aren't an ideal candidate for conversion to poetry. For starters, they're verbose. Even as prose, couldn't you say this:

> There was once a man who had three sons. The youngest of them was called Dullhead, and was sneered and jeered at and snubbed on every possible opportunity. (28 words)

as

> There was once a man with three sons. Dullhead, the youngest, was always sneered and jeered at and snubbed. (19 words)

The meaning is the same, isn't it?

Here's my attempt at converting the opening lines of "the Golden Goose" into a poem by rewriting them while preserving their meaning. Most of the changes are bolded:

> The man ~~**once was a man**~~
> **had** three sons,
> ~~**Dullhead,**~~ the youngest,
> ~~**was**~~ **always** sneered **at** and jeered at
> and snubbed.
> ~~**on every possible opportunity**~~.
>
> **When** the eldest son went into the forest
> to cut wood,
> His mother gave him a fine cake and a bottle of wine,
> so that he might be sure not to suffer
> from hunger or thirst.
>
> ~~**In the forest**~~, he met a ~~**little old**~~ grey **little** man
> ~~**who wished him**~~ "Good-morning," **he** said:
> "Do give me a piece of your cake
> and a draught of your wine—
> I am so hungry and thirsty."

A clean version:

> The man
> had three sons,
> the youngest
> always sneered at and jeered at
> and snubbed.
>
> When the eldest son went into the forest
> to cut wood,
> His mother gave him a fine cake and a bottle of wine.
>
> He met a grey little man.
> "Good-morning," he said:
> "Do give me a piece of your cake
> and a draught of your wine—
> I am so hungry and thirsty."

Notice that this version dispenses with the giveaway storytelling quality of "There was once…" and "one time…" It condenses the language, removes Dullhead's name for the time being— "Dullhead, the youngest," is explanatory in a prose-like way—exchanges the prose-like "a little old grey man" for the more rhythmic and less literal "grey little man." It also creates rhythm through lines like "**al**ways **sneered** at and **jeered** at/and **snubbed**." Rhythm is created by different means in the last stanza: each line has more or less the same number of syllables. More on this next week.

Make clear to the student that this exercise will gain a lot more depth next week, when we bring accenting into it. The da-DUM of emphasis adds far more to sound than sheer syllable count. But I wanted to separate the challenge into two lessons at this early stage of our study of meter.

You may wish to revisit the haiku lesson in Year 2 (Week 12) for its practice of syllable counting without concern for emphasis. You may also wish to revisit the one-line poem exercise from two weeks ago for a refresher on the creation of single lines that tell as much of a complete story as possible. It's not mandatory this week to tell a complete story, or even complete a sentence, with each line of poetry: "And then I said to the doleful walrus" is a perfectly acceptable line.

After reviewing the basics at howmanysyllables.com, go through the writer's randomly chosen 20 to see first-hand how the rules apply. You may wish to start with two-syllable words, but then branch out to longer words. If the writer's random selection didn't net longer ones, return to the dictionary to pick some out.

When the writer is ready to compose his 10 lines, you may wish to go back to several poems or snippets he has already written this year, and count how many syllables appear in those lines. (Those lines, or slight modifications of them, are not eligible this week.) This is a way to show the writer that he has already performed the assigned task. The difference this week is that he is being asked to become aware of one aspect of the crafting.

If the writer is struggling to come up with single-line ideas, here are several 10-syllable lines. Feel free to chop them off midway and ask the writer to finish them.

1. "Wor-ship be-gin-nings," the pro-fes-sor said. [I really did have a professor who taught us to pay special attention to the way we began our works, so that seemed appropriate here. But my first draft of the line had "writ-ing teach-er"

in lieu of "pro-fes-sor." That was one syllable too many, so I adjusted, but my first step was to just get the basic idea down. Then the writer can worry about tweaking in order to arrive at 10 syllables.]

2. The world is flat, as eve-ry per-son knows. [I had a similar challenge here, though my total was two short instead of one over; the original had "eve-ry-bod-y" instead of "eve-ry per-son."]

3. Your mag-nif-i-cent hum-ming-bird fin-gers.

4. Un-der-neath the can-o-py, the rooks squall.

5. Ten syl-la-bles! There is bet-ter home-work.

There is an infinite number of challenge exercise variations to assign here, but let's not forget our main task: to get the writer to appreciate how a certain kind of regularity in meter (syllable count and accent) can affect the sound of a poem. Meter isn't as customary as it was once, but it *is* deployed, if more selectively and less strictly. Either way, it's essential to understand, in part because so much great poetry was written in meter. Before something can be dismissed, it has to be learned.

The key thing to convey to the writer is that accenting in poetry works differently than it does in the English language. It's not about what the dictionary says—it's about what the line is trying to say, and where the emphasis goes as a result. More than any other lesson, this one's all about *saying it out loud*. There may be several different ways to validly accent it.

Make sure that the writer's examples of monometer include both single two-syllable words and two single-syllable words. With dimeter—four syllables—you can have anywhere from one word to four. With trimeter, from one word (a challenge) to six. And so on.

If the writer is struggling to come up with examples, listen around yourselves: to television slogans, to captured talk, to the lines in a newspaper. Enunciate these phrases together with the writer and practice assigning stress (either by drawing an accent or underlining the stressed syllable). These sources should give the writer a starting idea, from which he can tweak as I did last week. Having to fit patterns of meter is also a great exercise in synonyms, concision (or expansion), revision, and so forth.

In Challenge Exercise #1, the Shakespeare sonnet is written (mostly) in iambic tetra meter—accented syllables precede unaccented regularly, but in lines of eight syllables, not 10, However, there are some (underlined) exceptions. (Rhyme scheme to the right of the poem.)

Those **lips** that **Love's** own **hand** did **make**	a
Breathed **forth** the **sound** that **said** "I **hate"**	b
To **me** that **lan**guish'd **for** her **sake**;	a
But **when** she **saw** my **woeful** **state**,	b
Straight in her **heart** did **mer**cy **come**,	c
Chiding that **tongue** that **e**ver **sweet**	d
Was **used** in **giv**ing **gen**tle **doom**,	c [near-rhyme]
And **taught** it **thus** a**new** to **greet**:	d
"I **hate"** she **al**ter'd **with** an **end**,	e
That **fol**low'd it **as** gentle **day**	f
Doth **fol**low **night**, who **like** a **fiend**	e [near-rhyme]
From **hea**ven to **hell** is **flown** a**way**;	f
"I **hate"** from **hate** a**way** she **threw**,	g
And **saved** my **life**, **say**ing "not **you**."	g

For a wonderful, readable analysis of the meaning and meter of the poem, check out: poemshape.wordpress.com/2009/01/07/sonnet-145-shakespeare-iambic-tetrameter/

Lines 5, 6, 12, and 14 are the odd men out.

Line 5: "Straight" is a meatier word than "in." It gets the stress. And then we skip over "her" for the meatier "heart" to get the accent. In other words, the line returns to iambic tetrameter.

Line 6: The first syllable in "chiding" gets the accent, not the second. Again, we skip over "that" for the meatier "tongue" to get the accent. The line returns to iambic tetrameter.

Line 12: Same goes for "heaven." "Hell" is meatier than "to"—it gets the next accent.

Line 14: "Saying" briefly disrupts the meter because the first, not the second, syllable in the word is accented.

Ask the writer if he can identify the "irregular" meter in Lines 5, 6, 12, and 14. The opening feet in Lines 5 and 6 are **trochaic**: Stressed followed by unstressed. In line 12, we have an **anapest** – two unstressed syllables followed by a stress – before the meter returns to iambic tetrameter. In line 14, we have another **trochee**.

You can also practice rhyme with the writer by asking him to render the rhyme scheme.

POETRY • WEEK 13 • MENTOR'S NOTES

There's ample guidance in the lesson.

POETRY • WEEK 14 • MENTOR'S NOTES

This exercise can be a lot of fun, not to mention that it can teach the writer a couple of words for her next trip abroad. Foreign words whose meanings we know can make an English-language poem that much more poignant and striking. Foreign words whose meanings we *don't* know will lead us to wonderfully absurd results that would be hard to emulate "on purpose" (the mind gets too much in the way). This latter approach simulates the kind of mind-setting-aside the advanced poet must master: he must often ignore meaning for sound, and reason for instinct.

If the writer is struggling to come up with a poem in English, she can use an already-written one from this year or a previous level, or even one of the published poems we've looked at. "Feared Drowned" with Mandarin vocabulary? That would be interesting.

Poems have sensibilities that are sometimes indivisible from the places they were written. Both Walt Whitman's "1861" and Robert Frost's "Mending Wall" are profoundly American poems, not only because of what they're *about*—the Civil War and rural Northeastern life—but because of their style, the vivacious exclamation of the former and the steady progress of the latter. A discussion of "national" strains in French and German poetry is outside the scope of this book, but suffice to say that inserting a word in German, where the nouns are capitalized, or Russian, where there are practically no silent letters, alters the dynamic of a poem, even if ever so slightly. Depending on the writer's interests in language and culture, these subtleties may be interesting to discuss.

As for how to proceed after the writer has chosen a poem:

1. Pick out words to cross out. That should be fun. Words like "of" or "the" are less meaningful to sub than fleshier, more substantive choices like nouns and adjectives.

2. Find a source of foreign-language words. It might be fun to poke a finger at the map, then find the website of the capital's newspaper for that country. Another fun alternative is to use words from a themed source, like a cookbook, yielding a wacky kind of constancy to our lines, such as (using Portuguese again):

   What a *pate-de-azeitonas* [olive-dip] moment,
   The first day of *mariscos* [shellfish] when the sun doesn't appear.

   Pick the needed number of words (one per line) at random, or go one by one, using whatever guideline the writer would like: If she's replacing an adjective, she can "search" for what feels like an adjective. If she's looking to replace a word of exclamation, she can look for a word that feels exclamatory.

   It's important here to ask the writer why she is choosing the word that she is, if she's not choosing it randomly. It's not about picking correctly; it's about getting the writer to articulate what feelings the look and sound of a certain word inspire.

   The Five Senses exercise for English words in a previous level of this series asked writers to come up with associations for English words using the five senses: Forgiveness tastes like, sounds like, etc. The very same is possible with words in a foreign language. If the writer has encountered a word she is particularly drawn to, do the Five Senses exercise with it.

3. After the writer has made her substitutions, she can look up the words, and recreate the poem in English, sparking some laughs and groans, no doubt.

   And so she will end up with three documents:

   a. A poem in English
   b. A fresher, more surprising version of the poem with foreign-language confetti
   c. A reconstituted, absurd version of the English poem

This exercise blends several tasks the writer has received before: The exercise that asked him to come up with a name for an invented country and its national symbol; last week's work with words of unfamiliar meaning; last year's exercise asking the writer to make a poem out of English words he didn't know. This exercise takes things a step further by asking the writer to come up with a whole poem's worth of words from scratch. Next week's exercise will take this challenge even further by asking the writer to compose a whole poem out of invented words.

When a poet looks for words in his poem, he chooses among words that may mean similar things by their sound. That's what the variation in the first part asks: What word would *sound* right here?

The second part of the exercise tries to get the writer to experience the word even more closely—the look, the shape, the feeling—in an effort to invent a definition for it. This is an extension of the Five Senses exercise and a precursor to this year's penultimate assignment—translating a poem from a foreign language the writer doesn't know.

Part 1:

If the writer is struggling to invent words, play a game: take several words from the newspaper, choose a syllable from each (good syllable practice, too), and combine into a new word. Voila! An invented word.

Another fun game is to ask someone else to call out the first seven (or three, or ten) letters that come to mind. (Repetition allowed.) Just as in Scrabble, make a word out of as many of those letters as possible. The reason this is better than Scrabble? It doesn't have to be—*shouldn't* be—a real word!

For a great example of a poem that uses about one invented word per line (except the first and last four lines, which use mostly invented words), take a look at "Jabberwocky" by Lewis Carroll. I'll be discussing it with the writer in more detail next week.

Part 2:

If the writer is struggling to come up with definitions for the invented words, you can prod him with several questions:

1. Does the word sound like another whose meaning you know?
2. Does the word give you a feeling of any kind?
3. Do the letters resemble any shapes?

It may be quite tough to write a poem accommodating invented words with presumably unrelated definitions. In this, the exercise resembles one of the assignments related to the "captured dialogue" exercise: To find a way to make a poem out of so many random lines. Hopefully, you and the writer both saw the power of non-logical flow in poetry. This exercise is another way of enacting it.

Find online the opening six lines from the poem "Mottled Tuesday" by the great American poet John Ashbery. Can you make sense of them? Probably not. (I certainly couldn't.) What, then, is the point of reading poetry like this? Well, the sound of it. It's like a kind of music, like the words in a song. Think about it—when you listen to a song, often you pay only faint attention to the meaning of the lyrics. Sometimes, you don't even know what the words are exactly. You know them better as sounds.

So I listened to Ashbery's opening lines as I would to a song: the alliteration of "home" and "here," the echo of the d's in ran*dom* and plea*ding*; the longer opening lines giving way to the more rapid-fire delivery of the last two.

Both reading and writing such poetry is valuable, hence this week's exercise, which takes the writer's practice of pure sound further than before. You could help the writer get in the mood of invention by watching together a foreign film with the subtitles turned off. Most of the foreign films available in the U.S. have subtitles, but you can hang a towel across the bottom of your screen to hide them. It may be tormenting to watch a film without much idea of what's going on, but it's a great way to stop worrying about what the film means and just listen to the sound of the words, albeit with a little training-wheels assistance from the visuals. (And don't feel obligated to watch the whole thing.)

Need some suggestions? *Burnt by the Sun* (Russian), *Taste of Cherry* (Iranian), *Cinema Paradiso* (Italian) are all wonderful. The same thing goes for songs in foreign languages. Have the writer listen to a Spanish-language song by Gloria Estefan or Shakira, a Russian one by Vladimir Vysotsky, or an Italian one by Adriano Celentano. (YouTube makes this easy.) Any time the writer catches or thinks of a word he likes— likely to happen—ask him to jot it down.

The writer has several approaches from which to choose, as listed in the lesson. The bigger challenge than last week is that coming up with a single word won't do. That word has to become part of a line that has at least some understanding of rhythm, accent, etc. It may be worthwhile to review the meter lessons from the previous section. The writer doesn't have to come up with perfect 10-syllable lines, but as he saw in the lesson, certain word combinations work better than others. This exercise isolates that.

Make sure the writer reads everything aloud. If the line sounds like a mouthful, ask him to modify it by removing a syllable from a word, or cutting a word altogether. It's certainly a restriction to have to write a poem without knowing the meanings of the words, but the upside is the writer can tweak any word at will.

Who knows: one day, this exercise may be responsible for the writer's screenplay about an alien race that speaks a *very* poetic tongue.

What is the value of this exercise? To intensify and expand our practice with the feelings inspired by sound, without interference from meaning.

Make sure the reader has both read the poem (aloud and to herself) and had it read to her. Ask her if the poem as a whole inspires any feelings. Ask her to listen to the poem another time, jotting down any images that come to mind, even those that seem random or unconnected. What did it make her think of?

You can move to specific words. Pick one of the words and say it aloud 10 times. What associations does it bring up? What does it make the writer think of?

After enough practice of this sort, the writer will have a thread she'll wish to unspool in a full translation. That translation is likely to have nothing to do with the original, and that's fine. The goal is to translate our feelings about sounds into the translation. It's actually a new poem, not a translation, but one inspired by sound rather than meaning. Think about it: every time the writer sits down to work on a poem, the starting point is "what should it be about"? Not "how should it sound"? The poem-in-an-invented-language and this exercise explore sound as the *motivation* instead. Of course, even poems started by "What should it be about?" can be aurally sophisticated. A good poet writing a poem about an unrelenting rain will subconsciously choose words that evoke the sounds of the situation. But pure sound practice is just as valuable.

POETRY • WEEK 18 • MENTOR'S NOTES

No supervision this week. Let the writer explore freely. (So long as she does the assignment, of course!)

Appendix A[15]

Goold Brown's lecture on sound

CLASSES OF THE LETTERS

The letters are divided into two general classes, *vowels* and *consonants.*

A *vowel* is a letter which forms a perfect sound when uttered alone; *a, e, o.*

A *consonant* is a letter which cannot be perfectly uttered till joined to a vowel: *b, c, d.*

The vowels are *a, e, i, o, u*, and sometimes *w* and *y*. All the other letters are consonants.

W or *y* is called a consonant when it precedes a vowel heard in the same syllable; as in *wine, twine, whine*; *ye, yet, youth*. In all other cases these letters are vowels; as in *newly, dewy, eye-brow.*

CLASSES OF CONSONANTS

The consonants are divided into *semivowels* and *mutes.*

A *semivowel* is a consonant that can be imperfectly sounded without a vowel, so that at the end of a syllable its sound may be protracted; *l, n, z, in* al, an, az.

A *mute* is a consonant which cannot be sounded at all without a vowel, and which at the end of a syllable suddenly stops the breath; *k, p, t,* in *ak, ap, at.*

The semivowels are *f, h, j, l, m, n, r, s, v, w, x, y, z,* and *c* and *g* soft. But *w* or *y* at the end of a syllable is a vowel. And the sound of *c, f, g, h, j, s,* or *x* can be protracted only as an *aspirate*, or strong breath.

Four of the semivowels—*l, m, n,* and *r*—are termed *liquids*, on account of the fluency of their sounds; and four others—*v, w, y,* and *z*—are likewise more vocal than the aspirates.

The mutes are eight: *b, d, k, p, q, t,* and *c* and *g*-hard. Three of these—*k, q,* and *c*-hard—sound exactly alike. *B, d,* and *g*-hard stop the voice less suddenly than the rest.

15 Goold Brown, *Brown's Grammar Improved.* New York: Samuel S. and William Wood, 1860, pp. 20-21.

Permissions

Farrar, Straus, and Giroux, LLC: "Ponies" from *Collected Poems* by C.K. Williams. Copyright © 2006 by C.K. Williams. Reprinted by permission of Farrar, Straus and Giroux, LLC and Bloodaxe Books.

Joseph Hutchison: "Artichoke," by Joseph Hutchison, used by permission of the author. Copyright Joseph Hutchison 1985.

Random House, Inc: *The Autograph Man* by Zadie Smith. (Random House, 2002; Penguin Books, 2003). Copyright © Zadie Smith, 2002. Reprinted by permission of Random House and Penguin Books.

The University of Pittsburgh Press: "Feared Drowned" from *Satan Says*, by Sharon Olds, © 1980. Reprinted by permission of the University of Pittsburgh Press.

The Wylie Agency, LLC: Excerpt from "William Faulkner, The Art of Fiction No. 12," an interview by Jean Stein, Issue 12, Spring 1956. Copyright © 1956 by *The Paris Review*, used by permission of The Wylie Agency LLC.